Internet Resumes

Books by Peter D. Weddle

Career Fitness: How to Find, Win and Keep the Job You Want in the 1990's

Computer-Based Instruction in Military Environments

Electronic Resumes For the New Job Market

Internet Resumes: Take the Net to Your Next Job!

ROI: A Tale of American Business

INTERNET RESUMES
TAKE THE NET TO YOUR NEXT JOB!

Peter D. Weddle

IMPACT PUBLICATIONS
Manassas Park, VA

Copyright © 1998 by Peter D. Weddle

Library of Congress Cataloging-in-Publication Data

Weddle, Peter D.
    Internet resumes : take the net to your next job! / Peter D. Weddle.
        p.   cm.
    Includes bibliographical references.
    ISBN 1-57023-094-3 (alk. paper)
    1. Resumes (Employment)—Computer networks. 2. Job hunting—Technological innovations. 3. Job hunting—Computer networks.
    4. Internet (Computer network) I. Title.
    HF5383.W327   1998
    808'.06665—dc21   98-17710
                                                              CIP

For information on quantity discounts, Tel. 703/361-7300, Fax 703/335-9486, or write to : Sales Department, IMPACT PUBLICATIONS, 9104-N Manassas Drive, Manassas Park, VA 20111-5211. Distributed to the trade by National Book Network, 15200 NBN Way, Blue Ridge Summit, PA 17214, Tel. 800/462-6420.

Contents

PART I
How to Write an Electronic Resume

v

PART II
How to Write an Internet Resume

The Author

Peter D. Weddle is a businessman turned author and commentator. Described by *The Washington Post* as "... a man filled with ingenious ideas," he has earned an international reputation exploring business and career issues in the post-industrial era.

His business career spans more than twenty-five years, including ten at the CEO and Board level. He has led two international human resource consulting firms, a not-for-profit human services delivery organization and a start-up research and publishing company. He also founded and later sold Job Bank USA, Inc., a pioneering electronic employment services firm, which was endorsed by over 400 professional and trade associations, alumni groups and other affinity organizations.

A full time professional writer since 1996, he has authored four books, edited two others, and had dozens of articles published in professional and trade magazines. He writes a weekly review of Internet employment sites which appears in both the print and on-line editions of *The National Business Employment Weekly*, published by Dow Jones. He also writes and publishes two newsletters: one for employers, called *Weddle's Wildly Useful, Up-to-the-Minute Newsletter about Internet Resources for Successful Recruiting & HR Management*; and one for job seekers, called *Weddle's Wildly Useful, Up-to-the-Minute Guide to Internet Resources for Successful Job Search & Career Management*. In addition, he is often invited to speak about work and career issues and has addressed the national conventions of major associations and annual corporate meetings and appeared on radio and television programs all over the country.

For

My Mother & Father

Introduction

The Unique Features of This Book

There are dozens, maybe even hundreds of resume books on bookstore shelves these days, so why use this one? In fact, there are even two or three other books out there about writing a resume for use on the Internet. So, what is it about this book that makes it different and special?

Internet Resumes is unique in three important ways:

- First, this book is organized according to **your** priorities. It covers the information that you want to know before anything else. In short, it begins by showing you how to write two state-of-the-art high tech resumes. One is known as an Electronic Resume; the other is called an Internet Resume.

  Most books about resumes for on-line use begin with an elaborate introduction to the Internet, optical character recognition technology, and the changing workplace of the post-industrial era. All of this information is helpful and relevant to the topic, but for many job seekers, it's far more background and introductory material than they want. What they are really looking for is an easy-to-use, step-by-step process which will help them to write a resume that will work effectively on the Internet. Consequently, that's exactly how I've presented the topics in this book. First, I tell you how to write two powerful, new versions of your resume, and then, I explain how and where to use them successfully.

- Second, this book does not contain long lists of on-line employment sites where you can put your new Electronic and Internet resumes to work. Currently, there are over 11,000 such sites operating on the Internet and the World Wide Web and more are being added every day. In fact, in any given year, as many as one-third of all existing employment Web-sites start operation, cease operation or change in some significant way. Hence, any list of these sites is both out of date the moment the book containing them is published and, potentially, the source of much frustration and wasted time as you visit one after another, trying to find the best site for you.

  On-line employment sites are the most exciting, new job search and career management resource to come along in the last decade, but to capture their benefits, you have to make smart choices among sites. Therefore, instead of laundry lists of undifferentiated sites, this book tells you how to (a) find sites on the Internet, (b) determine what information, services and products they offer, and most important, (c) evaluate their quality and potential usefulness to you. In other words, you'll have the knowledge you need to make smart choices about employment Web-sites, now and for the rest of your career.

- Third, this book will give you an in-depth look at some of today's best on-line sites. **It will help you to find the best resources available on-line at this very moment so that you can put them to work in your job search right now**.

  Every week, I write a review of Internet employment sites called—yep, you guessed it—the "Web-Site Review" which appears in *The National Business Employment Weekly*, published by Dow Jones. Every other week, I write my own newsletter for Employment Managers and recruiters, helping them to use the Internet to find the candidates they need for their employer's position vacancies, on the Internet. In researching and writing these pieces, I've acquired a great deal of information about what job search and career management resources are available on-line and which employment sites offer the best products and services for job seekers. I've used this knowledge to give you a special, insider's guide to 20 of the top sites that consistently provide superior services and support to working men and women, whatever their occupational fields.

Further, I periodically publish an update to these reviews in a private newsletter. Called *Weddle's Wildly Useful, Absolutely Free Guide to Internet Resources for Successful Job Search and Career Management* or just *Weddle's,* for short, it includes reviews of additional sites as well as other resources for tapping the power of the Internet to help you find a new or better job. You can receive this newsletter at no charge, via e-mail. Just send your name and e-mail address to me at my e-mail address:

pdweddle@worldnet.att.net

We'll add your name to the subscriber list right away.

Thanks and good luck with your Internet resume, your electronic resume and your on-line job search!

Peter D. Weddle
May 15, 1998

Internet Resumes

1

The Era of High Tech Resumes

During the fifty years between the end of World War II and the middle of the 1990's, the techniques for finding a job scarcely changed at all. Basically, you wrote a paper resume, looked at the classified ads in your local newspaper, sent your resume through the mail to employers with job openings of interest to you and networked with friends and colleagues over lunch and the phone. It was a time consuming, laborious and often expensive process, but it usually worked.

Then, in the late 1980's, something happened. A little known network of research computers was transformed into a global "information superhighway," and the way organizations accomplished their work and conducted their business changed forever. Corporate communications, retail sales, inventory management, meeting planning, education and training, product design, team meetings and actual product development, all of it and more began to occur in cyberspace, on the Internet and the World Wide Web. Today, less than a decade later, millions and millions of organizations are on-line and using the Internet to conduct business and perform key functions!

It is a revolution in the world of work and, not surprisingly, it has also profoundly altered the way you find a job and manage your career. For the first time in fifty years, job search has moved beyond the staid, old realm of

1

paper resumes and the post office. It has been automated with advanced computer technology and burst onto the Internet, creating a whole new dimension for exploring employment opportunities and building a success-ful career. No less important, the scope of that change continues to grow broader and deeper with each passing day. Here's the evidence:

- A survey conducted in 1998 by Management Recruiters, Interna-tional, an executive search firm based in Cleveland, found that 37% of companies now recruit on the Internet and World Wide Web, up from 26.5% just 18 months ago. More than 29% of companies now post jobs on their corporate Web-sites; a year ago, that number was too small to report.

- According to a report published by the American Management Association in 1997, 51% of all companies expect to be using the Internet to recruit by 1999.

- Similarly, the 1997 Forrester Report on Classifieds and Directories noted that employers are currently spending $48 million to recruit on the Internet, and projected that figure to grow almost ten fold— to an astonishing $460 million dollars—by 2002!

- And since results are the best indicator of what will stay and expand in business usage and what will disappear, consider this fact. A 1996 *Bulletin to Management*, published by The Bureau of National Affairs, reported that more than half of the companies it surveyed had filled at least one position with applicants sourced from the Internet. And that was over two years ago!

In short, to find the best opportunities in today's job market and build a successful career, you have to be able to connect with increasingly computer-dependent employers, in general, and with those which are using the Internet and the World Wide Web to recruit, in particular. And to do that, you must know how to write an Internet resume.

The High Tech Record

An Internet resume is a high tech record of your work experience and qualifications that is designed for use in cyberspace. In other words, its format is designed to enable the resume to travel across the World Wide Web and the Internet without being distorted or worse, lost among the electrons. Similarly, its content is organized and composed to ensure that the resume (and your credentials) will not be overlooked when employers search the computerized databases that both they and employment Web-sites use to find qualified candidates for their open positions.

The Internet resume also has an "electronic" variation. It enables your credentials to be transferred accurately from a traditional paper format to the digitized environment of computerized databases. Since a large and growing number of employers and employment Web-sites use such databases (more about that later), this version of the Internet Resume launches you into today's highly automated job market, even if you do not have access to the Internet or to a computer.

The Internet resume, in contrast, is specifically designed for on-line use. It enables you to transfer your occupational background and expertise to those employers who maintain home pages on the Internet and to the thousands of employment Web-sites that are now in operation. The Internet Resume is specifically configured to take advantage of the speed and timeliness of on-line communications and delivers your employment qualifications over the Internet and the World Wide Web without garbling or losing key elements.

The Electronic Resume

The electronic version of an Internet resume (which I will simply call an "electronic resume") is similar to a conventional resume in that it is a paper record of your occupational credentials and experience. However, its content and format are specifically designed to be compatible with a computer. That's important because computers are very single-minded. Unlike humans, they cannot make judgments or extrapolate from the information you provide. You cannot count on them to read between the lines or to assume something on your behalf. For a computer, either what you want to say is expressed in your resume in a way the computer can recognize or it's not. There's no "sort of's" or "maybe's."

An electronic resume compensates for these limitations by organizing and presenting your qualifications in a "computer friendly" format. It is specifically designed to be compatible with the sophisticated technology that is growing ever more prevalent in the world of recruitment. This technology is used by employers, employment agencies and search firms and by employment Web-sites.

- **Employers:** Human Resource Departments in organizations ranging from Fortune 100 corporations to much smaller companies use resume management systems to move the mountain of paper resumes they receive from employment candidates into a computer-controlled database where the resumes can be effectively stored and searched.

- **Employment Agencies and Search Firms:** To a lesser extent, these organizations are also turning to computerized databases to archive the candidate resumes they receive and/or collect in the course of their assignments so that they can be easily accessed and reviewed during future search work for employers.

- **Employment Web-sites:** Ironically, many employment Web-sites, particularly those operated by professional associations, trade organizations and other affinity groups, also accept paper resumes from candidates and use resume management systems to build the databases which they then offer to employers on-line.

This growing use of advanced technology among employers and recruiters places new demands on your resume. Even in this new high tech environment, your resume remains your calling card in the job market. If it does its job effectively, it will persuasively showcase your credentials and open the door to an interview with those organizations offering opportunities for which you are qualified. To achieve that objective today, however, your resume must be pleasing and informative to **both** the eye and mind of human recruiters and the software programs and computer systems that employers, employment agencies and search firms and employment Web-sites now use to manage resumes.

In other words, if you want to be visible in today's job market and considered for the best job openings, you have to have a resume that gets along with computers. That means the computer must be able to understand and accept your resume—so that your credentials get stored in its database—and the computer must be able to recognize the words you use to express those credentials—so that it will pick your resume out from all of the others in the database when you are qualified for a particular position. If the computer hiccups on either of those two functions, your resume may be a work of art and you may be just the person an employer is seeking, but the connection will never be made.

The unique design of an electronic resume enables it to avoid such a disaster. It incorporates a number of relatively simple, but very important changes to both the format and content of a conventional paper resume. First, the information in an electronic resume is laid out so that it can be easily processed by an optical character recognition system—that's a piece of technology that "reads" your resume and then inputs it into a computerized database where it is stored. If your resume can't get past this first step, it will almost certainly be stored in the other resume repository used by recruiters, the waste basket. Second, an electronic resume expresses your employment credentials with the exact words and phrases that recruiters use to tell their computers which candidates to select in the database. Your qualifications must be conveyed with this special vocabulary or your resume will not match the computer's criteria and you will not be identified as a qualified candidate. An electronic resume integrates both of these components into an unique "computer friendly" design that can put the power of recruiters' own technology to work for you.

While having such a resume is critical to success in today's job market, it does not mean that you must now use two different resumes—one for human recruiters and the other for their computers—in your job search. Indeed, electronic resumes have a much broader application than their use in computerized resume management systems. Their format and content are also effective in the "paper environment" that still exists in many employers' Human Resource Departments today.

This environment imposes its own set of demands on your resume. Budget cuts and decreased staff resources in these Human Resource

Departments have dramatically curtailed the time and level of attention that can be devoted to candidate resumes. Indeed, when a paper resume is received by an employer, whether in response to a recruitment advertisement or from an interested job seeker, it is now usually reviewed by a support staff person—often a receptionist or secretary—who must rapidly sort through this pile of candidate resumes to identify those individuals who are most likely to be qualified for further consideration. A survey by *U.S. News & World Report* found that the "average" Fortune 500 company receives over 1,000 unsolicited resumes every week, so this task, while important, is also a huge burden. As a result, it is estimated that a resume now receives as little as 15 seconds attention when it reviewed. If your resume doesn't catch the eye of the staff person then, your window of opportunity is likely to slam shut forever.

As you will shortly learn, the format of an electronic resume addresses this situation by getting the most important aspects of your credentials up front, where they are less likely to be overlooked. Unlike a conventional resume, it leads with your strength rather than burying your credentials in the dense text of the body of your resume, so that even an overworked staff person can't miss them. Hence, an electronic resume is a multi-purpose document that will serve you well in a number of different environments. These include:

- the computerized resume management systems that are increasingly used by large and small employers;

- the computerized databases of candidate resumes that a growing number of employment agencies and search firms now maintain;

- the computerized databases that are developed from paper resumes for use on-line by a significant number of employment Web-sites; and

- employers' Human Resource Departments where recruiters and support staff conduct the initial evaluation of candidate resumes.

Whether it's single-minded computers or overworked staffers, an electronic resume has the right content in the right format to showcase your qualifications for today's employment opportunities. Chapters 2 and 3 will describe these two important elements in detail.

The Internet Resume

An Internet resume is designed to be transmitted from any computer to any other computer on the Internet or the World Wide Web. It uses a format called American Standard Code for Information Interchange or ASCII (pronounced "askee") to present your qualifications in a way that is universally recognized by all computers, be they PC, Macintosh or Unix based, and by all word processing applications, whether the recipient is using Microsoft Word, Word Perfect or something else. In essence, the Internet resume will effectively take your qualifications anywhere in the global, on-line job market you want to send them. There's just one catch.

Because it is designed to operate with all computers, ASCII has a simple, basic structure that lacks all of the stylistic embellishments typically included in the format of a resume. In other words, an Internet resume has no bold lettering, no bullets, no italics, no tabs, no pictures or graphics and no special characters or symbols. It's simply plain, unadorned, generic text.

An Internet resume looks like the body of an e-mail message or the content of a document on your word processing system when you save it as "text only." It is always aligned with the left margin and will only accept the letters, numbers and symbols you find on the keyboard of your computer. It will print out not in the font you use on your computer, but in the font set on your recipient's computer. And in most cases, it is limited to lines of about 60 characters because that is the line setting on many Internet browsers and e-mail readers.

While not as eye-appealing as a conventional paper resume or even an electronic resume, this format is particularly versatile, enabling you to connect with on-line employment opportunities in a much more efficient and effective way. That's important because, as the data presented earlier confirm, the Internet is fast becoming a key resource for employers.

Typically, organizations use one or both of two approaches to Internet recruiting:

- **Employment Web-sites:** A growing number of employers now look for candidates for their open positions by searching the resume databases of employment Web-sites. As noted above, some of these sites will accept a paper version of your resume which they will then transfer into their computerized database on-line. That takes time and the process is fraught with error (unless you use an electronic resume). Felicitously, a large and growing number of these sites, particularly, those which serve a broad spectrum of employers and occupational fields, now permit you to send your resume directly to their resume database on-line. In some cases, you simply paste a copy of your Internet resume into a standard input form that is available at the site and in other cases, you paste a copy into the body of a standard e-mail message and send that to the site. In either case, your qualifications will be quickly and accurately transmitted to the Web-site so that employers will have access to them in the site's resume database.

- **Employer's On-Line Classified Advertisements:** A large and growing number of employers now post their employment opportunities on the Internet. Some have created their own Web-sites and post job openings there; others post them in the jobs databases of commercial employment Web-sites; still others post them in "newsgroups," which are bulletin boards maintained for and by persons with similar occupational interests (such as journalists or physical therapists) and in a small but growing number of cases, certain employers are using two or more of these approaches to publicize their openings in cyberspace. With an Internet resume you can respond to these opportunities by simply pasting your record into an e-mail message and sending it to the advertising organization. As a result, you get your qualifications in front of recruiters without delay and long before a paper resume will arrive through the mail.

The Internet resume enables you to send your qualifications over the Internet without garbling or worse, destroying your message. Equally as important, the Internet resume is designed with the right content. As with an electronic resume, most employers automatically store the Internet resumes they receive in a computerized database. Hence, an Internet resume also incorporates the same words and phrases that recruiters use to tell the site's computers which candidates to select in the database.

All-in-all, the Internet resume gives you several important advantages:

- **Speed:** Your qualifications arrive in seconds or minutes rather than the days or even weeks it takes a paper resume to be delivered by mail. As a consequence, you can effectively respond to employers' time sensitive requirements and get your credentials in front of recruiters as soon as their openings are advertised.

- **Accuracy:** You can send your resume to any organization with a job opening anywhere in the world and be confident that it will be received in a recognizable and readable form, whatever computer system or word processing application the recipient is using.

- **Cost Savings:** When you use an Internet resume to transmit your credentials, you eliminate the cost of reproducing your resume on paper and the postage required to send it through the mail.

- **Flexibility:** Your Internet resume is stored on your computer, so you can easily update it to reflect changes in your qualifications or tailor it to a specific job opportunity.

- **Staying Power:** Once an employer receives your Internet resume, it can be stored in a resume management system and considered over and over again for new position openings.

- **Value-Added Credential:** Your use of an Internet resume demonstrates your knowledge of the Internet and its capabilities—which is certain to be viewed positively by prospective employers in today's increasingly interactive world of commerce.

An Internet resume enables you to connect with the growing number of employment opportunities now available in cyberspace and to capture the advantages of on-line communications. As with the electronic resume, the keys to its success are effective content and its unique format. Chapters 6 and 7 describe these two important elements in detail.

PART I

How to Write an Electronic Resume

2

The Format of an Electronic Resume

As discussed in Chapter 1, the electronic version of an Internet resume is specifically designed for the resume management systems and automated databases that are increasingly used by employers, employment agencies and search firms and employment Websites. It enables you to create a paper resume with the right format and content to be effectively input into, stored by and searched with a computer.

The format of an electronic resume is strongly influenced by two factors. One deals with what happens BEFORE a computer searches a database to identify the resume of a prospective job candidate, while the other influences what happens AFTER the computer does its work. Between those two points—when the computer is actually being used to locate the resumes of individuals who are qualified for a job—it is the content of an electronic resume that is most important. (Chapter 3 addresses this subject in detail.) Nevertheless, your resume will never get to the point where it can be effectively evaluated by a computer, nor will it serve you well once a human recruiter enters the process, unless you pay careful attention to its format.

The Importance of "Before"

Before an employer can use a computer to read and evaluate your resume for position vacancies, the resume must be entered into a database. As noted earlier, most of the resume management systems and automated databases used by employers and recruiters today input resumes into a database with an optical character recognition system or "scanner." Basically, a scanner takes a "picture" of your resume and converts that image into digitized information which the computer can then understand and accept.

Scanners, however, are very fickle machines. They can translate your resume into the language of computers **only** if they can recognize and digest the words on your resume. It's a situation analogous to reading your handwriting; if the computer can "read" what you've written, it will store the information in its database. If it can't, however—if your resume looks like hieroglyphics to the computer—it will simply reject your resume, leaving you out of the cyber-job market.

The first step in writing a good electronic resume, therefore, is to design its format so that the computer can understand what you've written. The following guidelines will help you to develop this "computer friendly" design for your resume.

Length

An electronic resume should be limited to two pages in length. Some employers will accept more, but many will not. The point is that all organizations using resume management systems and computerized data-bases are trying to maximize the efficiency of their technology, and long winded resumes tie up more than their fair share of the computer's limited memory or storage space. Hence, the best way to ensure that your resume will be accepted by an employer is limit it to two pages, if at all possible.

Further, an electronic resume should not be printed front-to-back on a single piece of paper. Instead, print the pages of your resume on two separate sheets of paper. That way, the person operating the scanner can stack one page on top of the other and scan both into the system simultaneously. A resume that is printed on a single piece of paper, on the other hand, has to be scanned twice; once, for the front side, and then again for the back side. That slows the processing of your credentials—and increases the likelihood that it will simply be discarded.

To ensure that the two pages of your resume stay together during processing and in the computer, identify each as follows:

- Top or first page—Insert your name and contact information at the top of the page and centered, as shown below. Put your name in bold typeface. Include an e-mail address, if you have one, after your phone number and separated from it with a slash mark ("/").

James Q. Seeker
1106 North Spring Field Drive
Allentown, Pennsylvania 66026
705-874-3302/jseeker@aol.com

- Bottom or second page—Insert your name in bold typeface and Page Two at the top of the page, at the left hand margin, as shown below.

James Q. Seeker
Page Two

Use a paper clip—not staples—to hold the two pages of your resume together. Some scanners struggle with the holes and tears that are created when the staples are removed, as they must be for processing.

Paper and Ink

Don't bother with expensive heavy weights or colors of paper. The best paper color for scanning is white; the best ink is black. They provide the greatest contrast which, in turn, helps the scanner to recognize the letters and words. Remember, a computer cannot make guesses about what it sees, so blurs and smudges look like indecipherable gobbledygook.

For example, if you use a gray paper and black ink for your resume, it may look attractive to the human eye, but it presents an incredible challenge to that myopic scanner. And when it translates the word "engineer" on your resume into "enjunioneer" in the database, the computer simply won't understand. It thinks you are an "enjunioneer," and you can count on it to identify your resume for any job calling for that credential. Unfortunately, you can also be sure that it will never identify you for a job as an engineer.

To appreciate just how much a scanner's inability to read your resume can hurt you, take a look at the resume on pages 15 and 16. The individual it describes might be a very accomplished professional, but the scanned resume completely obliterates that fact. As a consequence, the computer cannot identify him/her as a candidate for an employment opportunity even though this person might be fully qualified for that opening.

If possible, have your electronic resume printed at a local copy shop or use a laser printer to print it out of your word processor. Either way, you'll get clean black letters on the paper of your resume, and that's the key to effective scanning. The darker and more solid the letters, the better. Do not use a dot matrix printer as the images most of these machines produce are not of adequate clarity or definition for the caliber of scanner used by most employers today.

For the same reason, always send **an original copy** of your electronic resume to the employer, employment agency, search firm or employment Web-site. Never send a photocopy; the quality of the images is just not good enough. In addition, do not submit your resume by facsimile machine, even if the employer gives you that option. Although it is now possible to fax a document directly into a computer, most Human Resource Departments do not have such technology. Hence, while faxing your resume will get it to the employer more quickly than through the mail, your resume will still have to be scanned once it arrives, and faxed resumes are virtually impossible to process accurately.

So, what happens? Since no employer can afford to take the time to type your resume into its computer, the resume that arrives by fax will be scanned as is, with the unfortunate results shown earlier. Alternatively, in rare cases, it will be returned to you with the request that you re-send it by mail, or more likely, it will be tossed out with the trash without any notification to you. The end result is, at best, a delay in your ability to get your credentials into consideration, and at worse, your exclusion from the pool of candidates being evaluated for open positions that you may be qualified to perform.

The best paper weight to use with your electronic resume is copy grade paper (20 lb.) or something slightly heavier, such as the grade typically used in off-set printing (60 lb.). This approach has two benefits. First, heavy

STEVEN D. SPOTTS
147 Brookmeade Drive
Pittsburgh, PA 15237
(412)367 2732

OBJECTIVE: d and MBA education.
nameering backgroun
Obtain a position with a company that utilizes my e

QuALIEFICATIONS:
Two years expen'eiice as production eiigmeer *Ln a large petrochenu'ral plant
n @rorimental treatment systems design
Two years expenence as process engineer in e VI cess markets
Two years expen'ence as industn'al marketing manager m OEK distributor, and
cherru'ca pro
Excellent Interpersonal and conunuru'cations skills; reconunended for future
supervisory and leadership positions
N113A education with emphasis on production management and'mdustn'al
marketing

PROFESSIONAL F XPERI LENCE:
Marketing Manager; CA LGON CARBON CORPORATION; Pittsburgh, PA;
1992 Present
Participated on @gh performance, self directed work team that commercialized new
catal@c activated carbon
product line within six months. Planned sales to exceed $4 MM in 1994.
Managed OEM, distn@butor, and chenu*cal process markets totaling $45 MM in
sales.
Developed marketing program targeted at hydrogen purification OEMs reswting
in $1 MM in sales to date.
Conducted ten new product feasibility studies; eight studies were pursued for
further development.
Published seven water treatinent tec@cal papers; presented four papers at national
trade shows.

Process Engineer; CALGON CAPBON CORPORATION; Piushurgh, PA; 1990
1992
DesiVied, started up, and provided operator training for 20+ carbon adsorption
systems for van@ous air and
groundwater clean up applications.

Designed @and managed manufacture of 40+ mobile vapor phase adsorber U4 *ts, each val at $40,000.
.ru ued
Provided troubleshooting and recommendations for adsorber related customer problems.
Conducted technical and safety training for intemal engineering and operations personn I,.,.

Production Engineer; DOW CHEMICAL USA; Plaquendne, LA; 1988 1990
Directed operations personnel, schedwed eqw'pment maintenance, and planned shutdown pr *acts for 350 MM
Oi
gallon per year benzene production facility.
Engineered six process optii ru'zation pr @ects that resldted'm annual sav@Lngs of $1.8 NM.
Oi
Implemented SPC prograi ns on four distillation towers; annual benzene production grew by 1.2 MM gallons.
@aged detailed enginesting, construction, and start up of $1.3 @ waste hydrocar-bon coll@on system for
reduction of plant waste and coi npliajice with plant outfall pe@tting.

EDUCATION:
M.B.A., UNIVERSITY OF PITTSBURGH; Pitisburgli, PA; July 1994
Cw,nulative GPA . 3.9 4.0

B.S., PENNSYLVANI[A STATE UNI[VERSITY; University Park, PA; 1987
Major . Cheii u*cal Eng'Lneeriiig
Cw nulative GPA: 3.1 4.0

COMPUTER:
Proficient use of mainframe and PC ba@ platfonns experienced va@th many simldation optinuzation, and statistical
software packages including Lotus 1 2 3, FORTRAN, @tab, ASPEN, and various Windows based apptica@ons.

AFFILIATIONS:
Society of Soft Dn@nk Technolo 'sts; Water Quality @ociation

CERTIEFICATIONS:
Eii 'neer In Training, 1990

paper may impress human recruiters, but it is particularly bothersome for employers using resume management systems. Some scanners choke on heavier weights of paper, while others are forced to process it more slowly. Hence, the safest course is simply to avoid using it. Second, the resumes of qualified candidates are often copied for circulation within a prospective employer's organization. In effect, the money you spend on the higher grade paper is lost the minute you become a viable candidate. At best, that investment will only impress two people: the person who first reviews your resume and the secretary who takes it down to the copier to reproduce it. After that, the weight and color of the paper play virtually no role in the review process. So, don't waste your money on fancy grades or colors of paper. Save it, instead, for your victory celebration after you've been offered the job.

Finally, most scanners can accept irregular sizes of paper, but some scanners cannot. Therefore, play it safe and use standard 8½ x 11 inch paper for your electronic resume. In addition, when you send it off to the job bank, send it **unfolded and flat** in a large envelope. The creases created when you fold a resume to insert it into a smaller, business (number 10) envelope destroy the clarity of its lettering, and as noted above, that spells trouble for the scanner.

Typeface and Graphics

The best typefaces for an electronic resume are those in which the letters are clearly separated one from another. When letters run together, either because of the style of the typeface or its size, a scanner will have problems reading them. Therefore, use a typeface that gives you distinct and separate lettering, such as Helvetica, Sans Serif or Times. The best font sizes are 10 to 12 points. They create letters that are large enough for most scanners to read and interpret, but not so large as to waste the limited space you have on your resume.

For the same reason, you should avoid most of the graphical techniques that are often used in conventional paper resumes to catch the attention of human reviewers. The scanner works best with simplicity so avoid the use of:

Technique	Problem in Electronic Resumes
italics, underlining, fancy typefaces	Scanners need clear, distinct characters or they will see blots and blurs rather than letters
columns or any other kind of land-scaping	Scanners read from left to right, so columns look like different pages of information to a scanner; also diagrams and pictures can confuse scanners, as these devices are designed primarily to read text
shading	Scanners need clear contrast between letters and background, so shading increases the likelihood of reading errors by a scanner
boxes	Computers are confused by the vertical lines in boxes which they may read as the letter "l"

Boxes are used in the text of this book to set aside examples for ease of reading. You should **not** use boxes to highlight material in a resume which may be scanned.

On the other hand, virtually all scanners can accept and understand bold lettering, so it is acceptable to use that one technique. As you will see below, however, I recommend that you confine your use of bold typeface to the titles of the major sections in your resume where it will enhance the appeal of your resume once it begins assessment by an organization's recruiters and the hiring manager responsible for a particular position vacancy. Indeed, I don't think the use of bold typeface is helpful at all in the text of your resume. Its only purpose there would be to emphasize an aspect of your resume, and scanners and computers are immune to such embellishments. Those single-minded devices read text, and whether it is bold or not will have absolutely no bearing on their recognition of the words or their importance.

If you follow the above guidelines, your electronic resume will have no problem being read and understood by a scanner, whether it is used by an employer to input resumes into a resume management system, by an employment agency or search firm to build its computerized candidate database or by an employment Web-site to transfer paper resumes into its on-line resume database. Once that happens, what does your resume look like inside the computer?

The Importance of "After"

The amount of machine memory required to store the electronic resumes in a computerized database is always limited to some degree or another. Consequently, most organizations use their scanners and optical character recognition technology to process candidate resumes into the computer in the tightly compacted format shown on page 22. This format takes up the minimum amount of memory possible in the computer and improves the efficiency with which the computer can search the database for prospective candidates. In essence, it has "less distance" to travel in order to read each of the words in each of the resumes in the database which is how it identifies the candidates who qualify for a particular position vacancy.

As you can see, all of the fancy spacing and lettering many people use on their resumes is completely lost in the processing which electronic resumes must endure. So, does that mean that the visual appearance of an electronic resume is not important? Absolutely not! As noted at the outset of this chapter, the format of your resume plays a key role **before** the computer reads it and evaluates your credentials for a job search—during its scanning and processing into the resume management system or database—and **after** the computer has read and identified it (and you) for a position vacancy.

In other words, once the computer has been used to locate your resume (because it describes qualifications specified by an employer), the resume will be extracted from the database and enter a conventional evaluation process. At that point, the organization's recruiters and hiring managers will conduct an assessment of what you can do and how well you can do it. To facilitate this review and show your credentials off to best advantage, therefore, your electronic resume must also be arranged to appeal to human eyes and tastes.

The format on page 23 provides the best arrangement with which to satisfy the fickle scanner, the single-minded computer **and** the human recruiter. It uses the following techniques:

- Major section titles and the names of your current and previous employers are set off in bold and in all capital letters.

- The titles of your current and previous positions are set off in bold and with initial capital letters (capitalize first letter in each word).

þ ®®TAMMY A. BEIL 510 Stonybrook Drive Norristown, Pa. 19403 (215) 630 4572 ®®SUMMARY OF QUALIFICATIONS Twelve years of successful sales and marketing management experience in health care, telecommunications and financial insurance industries Ability to quickly acquire thorough knowledge of products in virtually any industry Experienced in entrepreneurial enterprises Outstanding communication, organization and time management skills Strong interpersonal skills and ability to relate equally well to individuals at all levels of corporate structure ®®High levels of professionalism, integrity and dedication Strong work ethic initiative ®®EXPERIENCE Physicians Imaging Center, Bethlehem, Pa. 1 93 Present Marketing Manager Establish and maintain physician accounts for MRI centers Develop and execute market strategy for Bethlehem and Camp Hill locations ®®Manage and maintain the operations Bethlehem center ®®Increased Bethlehem center's production by 25% within the first three months ®®Assisted in establishing new market center in Camp Hill location ®®AT&T, Bala Cynwyd, Pa. 6 88 12 92 Account Executive, New Penn Del Branch ®®Recruited for position by Manager ®®Design and execute own market strategy ®®Rank in top 10% of sales among eighty colleagues in branch ®®Page 2 ®®Sell and maintain business account s in Southern Chester County and Montgomery County ®®Spent initial month in intensive corporate training program and marketing program ®®Equitable Financial Companies, Allentown, Pa. 9 85 6 88 Agent Registered Representative ®®Ranked in top 10% among 750 women agents nationwide and was invited to membership in "Raising Your Sights Women's Conference" ®®Attained Leaders Corporate Level of 1989 production (top 25% of entire sales force) ®®Made Maryland Educational Conference and Regional Sales Conference in 1986 ®®Marketed and sold life and disability insurance and equities to business and individual markets ®®Held 6, 63, 23 Security License ®®The Foliage Factory, Allentown, Pa. 5 87 7 89 Partner General Manager ®®Established and operated profitable plantscaping business (installation and maintenance indoor foliage for business establishments) ®®Major clients included AT&T, Lehigh University, Lafayette College, Allentown and other major hospitals, major area restaurants, law and electronic firms ®®Developed and implemented market plan and strategy ®®Held total personnel administrative responsibilities for all employees ®®Sold business to partner after relocation to Philadelphia area ®®Darrell Laboratories, Covina, Ca. 1982 1985 Distributor, Eastern Pennsylvania ®®Owned and operated this successful distributorship of vitamins and healthcare products, sold exclusively to physicians ®®Ranked fifth among twenty six distributors nationwide ®®Established and maintained client base of 200 physicians with whom excellent rapport was enjoyed ®®Page 3 ®®Capably executed purchasing, inventory, marketing, sales, recordkeeping, shipping and receiving functions ®®Distributorship dissolved when parent company changed exclusively to telemarketing sales ®®Other Experience ®®Cement National Bank, Manager Assistant 1980 1982 ®®Dr. Louis Sportelli, Chiropractic Assistant 1979 1980 ®®EDUCATION ®®The Pennsylvania State University, Great Valley, Pa. Masters of Management Business Administration Emphasis June 1990 15 Credits Fulfilled ®®The Pennsylvania State University, University Park, Pa. Bachelor of Science May 1980 Graduated with distinction and complete requirements for majors in Health, Physical Education and Biology Invited to membership in Golden Key and Lakonians National Honor Societies ®þ

Your Name
Your Mailing Address
Your Contact Telephone Number/E-Mail Address

KEY WORD SUMMARY:

This section contains the key words that a computer must see in your resume to consider you a qualified candidate for a specific position vacancy. A complete introduction to the Key Word Preface is provided in the next chapter.

EXPERIENCE:

MOST RECENT OR CURRENT EMPLOYER   Dates of Employment

Title of Your Most Recent Position   Dates in that Position
Describe the knowledge, skills and abilities you currently use or demonstrated in this position in a three-to-five sentence paragraph.
  • List one-to-three accomplishments, setting each off separately with bullets. Bullets must be filled-in and dark. Scanners will read hollow bullets as the letter "o."

Title of Your Next Most Recent Position
with the Same Employer   Dates in that Position
  • List one-to-three accomplishments, setting each off separately with bullets. Bullets must be filled-in and dark. Scanners will read hollow bullets as the letter "o."

NEXT MOST RECENT EMPLOYER   Dates of Employment

Title of the Last Position You Held With That Employer   Dates in that Position
Repeat the format above.

Title of the Next Most Recent Position With That Employer   Dates in that Position
Repeat the format above.

EDUCATION:

List your degrees, certificates, most important occupational training and licenses in this section.

PROFESSIONAL AFFILIATIONS AND AWARDS:

List all of your professional activities, to include the professional and trade organizations to which you belong and any leadership positions you held, key activities in which you participated and any awards or recognition you have received from these groups.

- Your accomplishments are set off with tabs and bullets, which must look like the bullet at the beginning of this sentence (i.e., be completely filled in) and not like the letter "o."

- A Key Word Summary begins your resume with a tight, complete listing of your key occupational credentials.

- The Experience section, detailing your occupational background, immediately follows your Key Word Preface, unless you are a recent school/college graduate. The tasks you executed, the functions you discharged and the achievements you accomplished in your work background are your most important qualifications for a new or better job.

- Sections describing your Education and Professional Affiliations and Awards follow the Experience section and conclude your resume.

No space is wasted with personal data or with such obvious statements as "References furnished upon request." The personal data leaves you vulnerable to biases and prejudices which, although illegal, still exist in the world of work. The references statement, on the other hand, uses space on your resume to say something that every recruiter already knows. It's very unlikely that you will be offered a job without your references being checked, so every qualified candidate, by definition, will have to furnish them.

If you're a recent school/college graduate, on the other hand, and don't have a significant work record, you should place your Education section in front of the Experience section in your resume, in order to highlight your competitive advantage in the job market: the currency of your occupational knowledge. Your most important qualification for that first job out of school is your exposure to and familiarity with the most up-to-date techniques, theories and principles in your field so get that credential up front where it's most likely to be noticed.

It should also be noted, however, that work experience, particularly in your intended field, is also very important for today's school/college students. Part time jobs during the academic year as well as summer positions and internships are key ways to acquire workplace skills and knowledge, even while you're a student. And that real world background will give you an important edge in your search for the best available job after graduation.

To summarize: the format of an electronic resume is clean, clear and crisp. It is effective and efficient in its use of space and lays out your credentials in a way that makes them easy for a computer to see, read and understand. Chapter 3 will present the guidelines for developing the content that will bring this format to life for both that computer and a human reviewer.

3

The Content of an Electronic Resume

As discussed previously, the unique computer-based resume processing and handling techniques of today's employers, employment agencies and search firms and employment Web-sites dictate a special design for the format of an electronic resume. Without that format, your resume cannot be efficiently or accurately entered into the computer or its database, and that situation, in turn, can jeopardize your ability to be considered for job openings.

The content of your electronic resume is just as critical to your success in today's increasingly high tech job market. Indeed, it is the content of your resume that determines its ability to describe and highlight your credentials and set you apart in a resume management system or a computerized database. Without the right content, the connections are broken between the employment opportunities at employers and employment Web-sites and your qualifications for those positions. When that happens, unfortunately, your resume will simply gather electronic dust in the computer, and you will lose your shot at the employment gold rush in cyberspace.

The Importance of Key Words

The content of your electronic resume is shaped by the way computers read text, in general, and resumes, in particular. Basically, they search for designated or "key words" by examining each and every word in each and every resume in its database. These key words are normally nouns or short phrases. They describe the knowledge, skills, abilities and experience that the employer must see in a person's resume to consider him or her a qualified candidate for an open position. When an employer or employment agency searches its own database for employment candidates or the database of an employment Web-site, the key words are usually obtained either from a position description or from an interview with the hiring manager. Some of the key words will be designated as requirements, without which a person cannot be considered a qualified candidate, while others may be viewed as capabilities that the employer would like to see in a candidate, but are not a precondition to hiring.

An electronic resume, therefore, is designed to present your occupational credentials using as many key words as possible. To get a feel for the key words that an employer might want to see in your resume, check the vocabulary in the recruitment ads for your field of work in your local newspaper. Look at the specific terms the employers have used to describe the knowledge, skills, abilities, competencies, capabilities, experience and background required for prospective employment candidates in your field. Alternatively, you can review the position descriptions that most employers maintain for the jobs in their organization. These documents are usually filed in the Human Resource Department and may even be posted for position vacancies.

In addition, you can also check with an executive recruiter or "head hunter" who specializes in your field. If he/she has conducted one or more searches recently for a position or positions similar to yours, the criteria for those searches will give you a detailed vocabulary of the most current key words in your field. Finally, you should check with your professional or trade association. If there is a certification or professional education program in that organization, it is likely to have instructional or testing objectives which will give you an insight into the latest key words of importance in your particular field.

Of course, your resume should include only those key words that describe qualifications that you actually have. In fact, think of key words as terms which describe your **ASSETS**. They are nouns or short phrases used to detail the **value** you offer to an employer. They include:

- **Abilities:** Any learned or acquired capability, expertise, knowledge, skill or competency that will enable you to perform your job at an exceptional level. Key words for abilities might include Budget Management, Operations Research/Systems Analysis, AS 4000 Programming, Oral and Written Communications Skills, Team Building, Sales Prospecting and IBM Word Processing.

- **Special Awards and Recognition:** Any recognition which you've received on-the-job or from your professional association that would indicate a special level of expertise, experience or commitment. Key words for awards might include Salesman of the Year, Quality Control Supervisors Award, MIS Department Top Performer Certificate, and National Management Association Distinguished Service Award.

- **Special Licenses and Certifications:** Any formal designation or title which you have earned via study, test, evaluation or other formal process conducted by your college or university, professional association, state or federal government or other recognized institution. Key words for special licenses & certifications might include SPHR (Senior Professional in Human Resources), CFP (Certified Financial Planner), Cum Laude Graduate, and Professional Engineer/License Number 123445.

- **Experience:** Your years of experience in your occupational field, industry, or management/skill level as well as any unique background with special projects, responsibilities, and activities. Key words for experience might include 14 Years in Plastic Industry, Progressive Development Through All Functions in Corporate Finance, Chairman for Special Environmental Compliance Project, 5 Years in Computer Sales and Administrative Assistant to Corporate Executives.

- **Training:** Any program of learning relevant to your performance on-the-job, to include high school, vocational school, college, in-house training and special educational programs. Key words for training might include Master of Science in Structural Engineering,

Motorola Total Quality Management Training, Associate of Arts in Administrative Science, Fluent in Spanish, Formal Training in Statistical Process Control, and Stanford Executive Development Course.

- **Synonyms:** Different people and organizations use different words to say the same thing. To account for this variability in human expression, your key words should include any alternative words, phrases or acronyms used to describe any of the key words in your resume. Illustrative key word synonyms are Personnel Administration for Human Resource Management, MA for Masters of Arts, Association or Society for Not-For-Profit, Attorney for Lawyer, and Supervisor for Manager.

Key words present **your assets** in **terms used by employers**. Why? Because those are the words and phrases recruiters use with their computers to search resume databases. If you have the right skill, but describe it with the wrong word, you'll be overlooked by the computer. It's as simple as that. So, there are only two criteria for selecting which key words to include in your resume:

1. they must be an accurate, honest expression of your qualifications, and

2. they must be the words and phrases used by employers to describe the qualifications required for a job opening.

Given these two criteria, the following additional guidelines will improve the quality and strengthen the impact of your electronic resume:

- It's perfectly all right to use acronyms in an electronic resume. If employers use the acronym to describe a required qualification, then it should appear in your resume. A word of caution is in order, however. If the acronym and its complete term are used interchangeably by employers, then **both** should appear in your resume.

- It's also okay to use jargon and detailed technical terms in an electronic resume, **if** employers use such words to describe required qualifications in your field.

Finally, you should avoid the use of soft, inexact or flowery language in an electronic resume. Employers do not use such terms as "empowerment" and "shirt sleeves manager" as key words when identifying the required qualifications for a position vacancy. These terms may make for pleasant reading, but they do not add important information to the resume and hence do not contribute to your evaluation by a computer.

The Key Word Summary

As noted in the previous chapter, an electronic resume begins with a Key Word Summary. This lead-off listing of your qualifications is a new technique specifically designed for an electronic resume. It operates as your own "electronic billboard," delivering the right information in the right place to highlight your employment credentials even in today's warp speed job market.

The Key Word Summary is a critical component of your resume for two very important reasons:

1. A growing number of resumes are being entered into computers by optical character recognition technology or scanners, and

2. Resumes are increasingly read by single-minded computers and overworked staff persons in employers' Human Resource Departments.

Even a resume with very strong content, one which includes all of the key words that describe your occupational credentials, can be overlooked if the arrangement of that information fails to address the impact of these two factors. Consequently, the key words in an electronic resume should be organized into two sections. The first is a Key Word Summary; the second is the main body of your resume.

The Key Word Summary appears directly beneath your name and contact information at the top of the first page of your resume. It is an up-front showcase of your most important ASSETS, as described by the key words you expect employers to use to describe your qualifications. The Key Word Summary is a list that includes twenty-to-thirty principal items, not including the articles and conjunctions (words such as "the," "and," "&," or "of") used to separate them. A principal item is the key word or phrase that describes a single and complete qualification. The first letter of the first word in the item is capitalized (unless it includes a title or an acronym, which is capitalized according to convention), and the entire item is followed by a period. For example:

Key Word Summary

Human resource management and development. Ten years experience in health care industry. Compensation & benefits. Employee relations. Staffing. Union relations. EEO/AA. Succession planning. Vice President of Human Resources for 1,000 employee company. SPHR.

The Key Word Summary acts as an inventory of the capabilities you can bring to an employer and as an advertisement about the quality of those capabilities. As an inventory, it includes the words that a computer or a recruiter must see to consider you a qualified candidate for a position vacancy. Basically, these words and phrases detail three aspects of your background:

- Your skills, abilities and competencies;

- Your experience using those skills, abilities and competencies; and

- Your accomplishments in using those skills, abilities and competencies on-the-job.

As an advertisement, the Key Word Summary is right up front where it can't be ignored or overlooked. It has the right words in the right place, whether your resume will be reviewed by a single-minded computer or an overworked recruiter. Hence, the Key Word Summary effectively and efficiently communicates **what you can do** and **how well you can do it**.

Following the Key Word Summary, the body of your electronic resume should be organized into three sections: Experience, Education, and Professional Affiliations & Awards. Each of these sections is described in detail below.

Experience

As with the Key Word Summary, the Experience section is an opportunity for you to document your occupational credentials. Hence, I believe that the best format for this section is a hybrid of the chronological and functional formats used in conventional resumes. The chronological format arranges your credentials according to your work history and presents them in chronological order, usually beginning with the most recent and working backwards to the most distant in time. A functional format, on the other hand, presents the occupational qualifications you possess and the experience you have had in building and using those capabilities.

Both of these formats have certain strengths and weaknesses. A chronological resume does a good job of detailing your work experience but may not provide adequate visibility to the knowledge, skills and abilities you have demonstrated in each position. A functional resume clearly overcomes that problem, but also makes it very difficult to determine what positions you have held, in what order and during which periods of time.

The hybrid format is widely used in conventional paper resumes because it eliminates many of these shortcomings, while capturing the best features of both formats. A hybrid format clearly presents your work history in chronological order **and** the knowledge skills, and abilities that you demonstrated in each position along the way. Hence, its only drawback is that you may not have the space, given the length constraint of an electronic resume, to cover every one of your prior work positions in detail. Nevertheless, I strongly recommend that you use the hybrid format because it best enables you to highlight your capabilities and experience in the key words that **both** a single-minded computer and an overworked recruiter will recognize and understand.

Indeed, introducing your capabilities is the single most important purpose of the Experience section. Organizations, today, are challenged by unprecedented competition in domestic and international markets and by escalating demands for improved productivity, quality assurance and customer satisfaction. To meet these challenges, employers seek workers who can demonstrate that they have both the background and the motivation to excel. In short, they want to hire winners because they know that their survival rides on the quality and commitment of their workers. The Experience section is the place in your resume where you can prove that you have this kind of background, that you have the right stuff.

The hybrid format organizes your experience around the progression of your employment positions, in reverse chronological order. In other words, the section describes each of the jobs you've held during your career, beginning with your most recent or current position. Jobs are arranged by employer, so the name of each organization and the dates of the entire period that you worked there are presented first. Then, the title of each of the positions that you held with that employer and the dates you held them are listed.

As shown below, names and titles are entered from the left hand margin, while dates are entered from the right. The names of your various employers serve as major section headings, so they should appear in all capital letters and bold type face. Position titles appear in initial capital letters (i.e., the first letter of each word is capitalized) and bold type face.

RESEARCH DYNAMICS CORPORATION	01/90-03/94
Department Manager	06/92-03/94
Regional Sales Manager	01/90-06/92

Beneath each position title, present additional information to supplement that which you listed in the Key Word Summary. This information should focus on **what you can do** and **how well you can do it**.

What You Can Do

The information beneath each position title should provide a mini-work history of the capabilities you demonstrated in the job, using the key words that single-minded computers and overworked recruiters will recognize and understand.

Limit yourself to a paragraph of three-to-five clear, hard-hitting statements. Don't talk about responsibilities, talk about capabilities—about what you can do, have done and will do for the employer. Hence, each sentence should identify either the major tasks you performed on-the-job or the skills and abilities you used to accomplish those tasks. And, remember, the vocabulary you use in these statements must be the key words or their synonyms that you developed for your Key Word Summary. In effect, the Experience section is the place where you present the proof. It's your opportunity to describe, amplify and confirm the details of the knowledge, skills and abilities you highlighted in the Summary.

That proof is critically important. Employers want to know **what you can do** for them. They hear a lot of claims and promises from job candidates, but not much of it gets taken very seriously. Instead, most organizations look for proof. They rely upon a very simple premise: if you've done something successfully in the past, you can probably do it again, maybe even better, in the future. Therefore, your "track record" of experience in the past is the single best way for you to impress an employer.

Treat each and every statement in the Experience section of your resume as an advertisement about you. To be effective, that ad should adhere to several principles:

1. **It must be accurate and honest**. No exaggerations, no misleading suggestions and certainly no misstatements of fact.

2. **It should leave nothing to the imagination**. As far as the employer is concerned, you didn't do it, if you don't say so. That's particularly true of electronic resumes. Remember, they'll be read by a single-minded computer which can't read between the lines and can't make a guess on your behalf.

3. **Your ad should be written for your audience**. You want to be sure that the audience recognizes and understands what you're telling them. For electronic resumes, that audience is a single-minded computer; and for all resumes, it is an overworked recruiter. Hence, your experience must be described using the key words and their synonyms for which computers and recruiters are looking.

By adhering to these principles, a good skills paragraph might look something like this:

> Recruited, trained and directed successful six person sales team for leading plastics manufacturer. Conducted comprehensive market analysis which identified key customer opportunities in the region. Reorganized sales territories to eliminate overlaps and focus on new account growth. Devised innovative sales prospecting and call-back strategy which helped agents develop effective customer relationships. Developed and personally implemented special handling procedures for improved management of all accounts greater than $1 million.

Remember, the goal here is to describe your capabilities in short, hard-hitting sentences that use the key words you think an employer will expect to see in the resume of any qualified candidate. However, as the paragraph above illustrates, the key words are neither presented in a laundry list nor enclosed in simple sentences that say nothing more than the fact you have such skills. In essence, your key word statements must also say something about what you can do **with** the capabilities and background those key words describe in order to be effective. For example, don't state "I was responsible for the development of sales strategy." Instead, say, "Devised innovative sales prospecting and call-back strategy which helped agents develop effective customer relationships."

To achieve that kind of impact, each sentence in the illustrative paragraph above has two parts:

1. The key words, themselves, which describe a specific, discrete capability, and

2. A precise, detailed description of the experience you had with that capability.

In addition, to be most effective, each key word statement should describe some improvement or contribution that was produced by your capabilities and actions. Remember, a prospective employer is looking for someone who can achieve beneficial results on-the-job. If you've been able to do that for one employer, there's a good chance you'll be able to do it for a new employer, as well. Each key word statement, then, should actually contain three elements:

1. The key words, themselves, which describe a specific, discrete capability, and

2. A precise, detailed description of the experience you had with that capability, plus

3. Some benefit or improvement you achieved for your employer.

The chart below identifies these three components in each key word statement in the illustrative paragraph.

Key Words	Experience	Benefit
team, plastics (industry)	recruited, trained, directed	successful
market analysis	conducted	identified key customer opportunities
sales territories	reorganized	eliminated overlaps; new account growth
strategy	devised, helped	effective customer relationships
procedures, $1 million accounts	developed, implemented	improved management

In summary, each paragraph in your electronic resume that describes your experience in a particular job should highlight the key words that identify the knowledge, skills and abilities you demonstrated in that position, the tasks or activities you performed with those capabilities, and the benefit or improvement those actions produced. Such a paragraph will provide you with two important advantages:

1. It can be understood by both single-minded computers and over-worked recruiters, and

2. It provides a meaningful, hard-hitting description of your capabilities and their application on-the-job.

Those two benefits will help determine whether or not you are identified as a qualified candidate for a particular position. They will not, however, differentiate you from the competition. They will not set you apart from all other qualified candidates who are competing for an employer's open position. To do that, you have to describe your accomplishments at work. In other words, each key word paragraph in your resume—if it's written well—will tell the computer or recruiter **what you can do** and some evidence of **how well you can do it**.

How Well You Can Do It

Perhaps the best proof you can offer regarding your knowledge, skills and abilities is the accomplishments you have achieved in using those capabilities on-the-job. Accomplishments describe the successful application of your competencies in real world, work situations. They provide some insight about your motivation, commitment and degree of expertise. Most importantly, they indicate a level of performance that you have already achieved and, therefore, should be able to repeat and build on for a new employer.

Indeed, accomplishments are so important that they should be set off from the text of your resume and highlighted for that single-minded computer and overworked recruiter. There are two steps you should take to do that. First, limit the number of accomplishments you present to no more than three per job. A long laundry list of accomplishments diminishes the impact of any single one, so be selective. Pick the two or three achievements that you feel best exemplify your unique capabilities and present only those. Second, limit the description of each accomplishment to a single punchy, fact-filled statement. Wherever possible, include quantitative measures of your success in your statements. Such empirical "evidence" provides more credibility and heightens the impact of your accomplishment.

Insert each statement beneath the paragraph corresponding to the position in which it occurred and set it off by bullets. Remember, the bullets on an electronic resume must be completely filled-in, like those below and not open which the computer will read as the letter "o." Therefore, an effective accomplishment statement might look like this:

- Increased sales by 20% per year over the past two years.

  or

- Lowered turnover rate among sales agents by 46%.

  or

- Improved key account renewal rate by 15%.

All of these statements demonstrate a capability, a task or action you can do on-the-job **and** how well you can do it. As shown below, when these statements of accomplishment are amended to their corresponding key word paragraph, they produce a complete picture of your experience in a particular position that has genuine power and impact. It's a portrait of you and your capabilities that will be understood and appreciated by both a computer and a human recruiter.

Regional Sales Manager
Recruited, trained and directed successful six person sales team for leading plastics manufacturer. Conducted comprehensive market analysis which identified key customer opportunities in the region. Reorganized sales territories to eliminate overlaps and focus on new account growth. Devised innovative sales prospecting and call-back strategy which helped agents develop effective customer relationships. Developed and personally implemented special handling procedures for improved management of all accounts greater than $1 million.
- Increased sales by 20% per year for the past two years.
- Lowered turnover rate among sales agents by 46%.
- Improved key account renewal rate by 15%.

Each description of each job you have held should be presented in just this way in the Experience section of your resume. By doing so, you provide enough content to attract the interest of a recruiter, in the key words that will be recognized by a computer. You are able to:

1. Qualify yourself as a candidate for a specific job opening by pointing out the principal knowledge, skills, and abilities you've used in your previous jobs and by demonstrating your application of those capabilities in the tasks and activities of your work, and

2. Differentiate yourself from the competition by highlighting your accomplishments in performing those tasks and activities on-the-job.

As further evidence of your capabilities, the next section of your resume should detail your educational credentials.

Education

The Education section in an electronic resume must be more complete and detailed than the same section in a conventional paper resume. That's because recruiters typically cite more than formal degrees and certificates as key words when using a computer to select qualified candidates. These additional key words cover a range of subjects, including (a) special training programs in such subjects as the C++ programming language, Total Quality Management, Statistical Process Control, Preventing Sexual Harassment, Working in Diverse Work Groups; (b) continuing educational experiences to acquire value-added skills in verbal and written communications in English, foreign language competency, and computer literacy; and (c) formal licenses and certifications.

All of these educational qualifications should be organized into an Education section with three distinct subsections:

- **First subsection**—the degrees and certificates you have earned from formal educational programs;

- **Second subsection**—the most significant training and continuing education experiences you have had during your career; and

- **Third subsection**—your formal credentials, licenses and certifications.

Recognizing that there is limited room for this information on your resume, I suggest that you keep a separate on-going record of **all** of your educational information (so that you'll have it handy for your interviews) and select one-to-three items from each area for actual inclusion in your resume. To select these items, use the following criteria:

1. The more recent (the degree, training, or license), the better, and

2. The higher (the degree, training level or license), the better.

The first subsection lists all of the formal education degrees or certificates you have received, beginning with the most recent first. These credentials signify your successful completion of a specific educational experience which will, in turn, provide further confirmation to a recruiter or computer that you possess the specific knowledge, skills and abilities required for a vacancy. They also underscore your capacity to stay with an activity and to see it through to successful completion. In other words, those degrees and certificates say something about your determination, your strength of character and your ability to get things done, all of which are important qualifications in today's demanding workplace.

List your degrees and certificates by their formal name, beginning at the left hand margin. Then, identify the corresponding educational institution which granted the degree or certificate, spacing its name roughly in the center of the page. This arrangement (i.e., degree first, then school) is reversed from that usually suggested for conventional resumes for a very specific reason. The degree or certificate is the most common key word used by single-minded computers and overworked recruiters to identify the required educational experience for a position vacancy. Moreover, humans read from left to right, so this arrangement puts the key words first, where they are most likely to be seen.

Identify your degree or certificate, using the most common key words **in your industry** for the degree (e.g., Masters in Public Administration, MPA, Masters in Business Administration, MBA, Doctor of Philosophy in Literature, Ph.D. in Literature, Associate of Arts, AA, Certificate in Paralegal Studies, High School Diploma, General Education Degree, GED). If you used the abbreviation in your Key Word Summary, then state the entire name for the degree in the Education section or vice versa. In addition, if you received the degree with honors (e.g., Cum Laude, Summa Cum Laude), note this distinction, as well.

Finally, indicate the date you received the degree, at the right hand margin. Some resume books will tell you to indicate the beginning date as well as the completion date of your degrees and certificates. While that information is nice to have, it takes up room on your resume and adds nothing of real importance to the credibility or strength of your credentials. In other words, the length of time you spent getting the degree is not nearly as important as how recent that degree is. The more recent the degree, the more up-to-date your skills, and that's precisely what the completion date will tell a recruiter or computer.

An illustration of the first subsection appears below.

Education		
Masters in Public Administration	American University	1979
Masters in Literature	Middlebury College	1978
Bachelors of Science	Fordham University	1971

The second subsection covers your most significant training and continuing education experiences. Your resume has greater strength if you indicate an on-going commitment to staying current in your primary occupational field and gaining new skills that can expand your contribution and impact on-the-job. Indeed, today, employers are more impressed with people who look like "works in progress" rather than "finished products," because they know that technology and strategies are evolving so rapidly that a person can only stay up-to-date if they are in school virtually all of the time.

Hence, this subsection of your resume is your chance to show that you accept the responsibility for and are committed to life-long learning. If possible, it should list training programs you have completed and those in which you are still engaged, limiting your list to those educational experiences that are relevant to your work on-the-job. This subsection is not the place to include that course in barn painting you took at the local community center, unless barn painting is an important addition to your qualifications for a certain job. The best rule of thumb is to include an education experience **only if** an employer is likely to identify the skill you acquire from that experience as a key word. How do you know? Check the newspaper employment section and talk to headhunters in your field.

Once you've selected the programs to include in this section, list the subject or title of the course, beginning at the left hand margin. As with your formal degrees and certificates, the subject of your training is far more important to a prospective employer than where you took the course, so it is identified first. Then, state where the course was taken, spaced roughly in the center of the page, and the date it was completed, at the right hand margin. If you're still completing the course, state "On-going" where the date of completion would have been entered. For example,

Education		
Masters in Public Administration	American University	1979
Masters in Literature	Middlebury College	1978
Bachelors of Science	Fordham University	1971
Conversational Spanish	Delta Community College	On-going
Total Quality Management	Motorola Quality Institute	1989

The final subsection of your Education section identifies your formal licenses, certifications and other credentials that convey a specific level of expertise recognized and valued by your industry and/or profession. Normally, such credentials require the successful completion of a specified course of instruction and a certifying exam, conducted either by your profession's designated association, society or institute or by the state or federal government.

List your licenses or certifications at the left hand margin. Remember to use the key words you think an employer would use to identify the qualifications for a position vacancy. Then, roughly in the center of the page, identify:

1. The state, institution or organization that awarded the license to you;

2. The number of your license, so that it can be confirmed by the employer; and

3. At the right hand margin, insert the date you received the license or the date it was most recently renewed.

For example,

Education

Masters in Public Administration	American University	1979
Masters in Literature	Middlebury College	1978
Bachelors of Science	Fordham University	1971
Spanish	Delta Community College	On-going
Total Quality Management	Motorola Quality Institute	1989
Professional Engineers License	Virginia #123456	1980
Senior Human Resource Professional	SHRM #109876	1986

The Education section in an electronic resume has to do more "heavy lifting" than a corresponding section in a conventional resume. The use of key words to search for and identify qualified candidates requires that the section expand to include any other special knowledge, training, licenses and certifications you may have. In addition, such an approach to detailing your educational experience will make an important statement about your commitment to continuous personal development, which can, in and of itself, help to differentiate you from the competition.

Professional Affiliations and Awards

This section is the last in the content of your electronic resume. It details your level of involvement, your stature and your standing in your profession, craft or trade. These credentials are important because they provide further evidence of your competency and your commitment to excellence in what you do. Hence, this section should detail your activities involving your professional or trade association as well as more general organizations related broadly to your work (e.g., the Chamber of Commerce, Young President's Organization, American Management Association), but not your alumni association, your Bird Watcher's Club or the Parent-Teachers Association.

In addition, the professional section of your resume should also include activities, events and accomplishments that are not related to a specific organization but which describe your on-going occupational development. These include professional papers and articles which you have published, speeches and workshops you have presented or independent projects you have completed.

In other words, limit entries in this section to those which are likely to

1. Be identified as a key word, or

2. Provide additional evidence that will help to differentiate the key words in your resume

Unlike the entries in the Education section, the names of the key professional or trade associations to which you belong should appear first in this section, beginning at the left hand margin. Given the wide range of possible levels of participation and recognition among these organizations, it is far more likely that the affiliation itself (i.e., the name of the organization) will be the key word either used by the computer or recognized by the recruiter.

For each organization you list, identify any leadership positions you held (e.g., Chairman of the Education Committee, Member of the Board of Directors, Chapter Chairman) or special activities you undertook on its behalf (e.g., Chairman of the Annual Conference, Member of Ad Hoc Committee on Dues). Also list any special awards or citations you've been given that would provide further evidence of your level of participation and recognition (e.g., Special Citation for Continuous Service) and their dates. In the case of papers you've published or programs you've presented, first cite the name of the publication or organization, then the name of your paper or presentation in quotation marks and the appropriate dates. For example,

---

Professional Affiliations & Awards

Society for Human Resource Management	Excellence in Education Award	1989
National Society for Performance & Instruction	"Training Generation X" Workshop	1991
Authors Guild	Admitted as Member	1991
Training Magazine	"How to Make Training Pay"	1994

Membership in and awards from professional and technical organizations in your field and participation in other developmental organizations and experiences related to your work are important indications of your commitment to high caliber performance and excellence in your occupation. They convey qualities of character—a sense of purpose and a dedication to personal accomplishment—that are highly regarded by employers everywhere. Hence, they are a fitting statement with which to close your resume.

Indeed, **do not** end your resume with such statements as:

Personal References Available Upon Request	The recruiter already knows that. In most cases, you won't be hired without them.
Married. Two Children. Member of Beth Shalom Temple. Episcopalian. Excellent Health. 52 Years Old. African-American. Asian-American. Caucasion. Male. Female. Handicapped.	These statements will almost never be key words for a position vacancy. They aren't relevant to your work, except in rare circum-stances. Besides, they can inadvertently expose you to illegal prejudice or bias in your job search. It's not supposed to occur, but why take a chance?
Enjoy sailboating, swimming, horseback riding, hunting, fishing, and so on. Active in Republican/Democratic Party.	These statements describe hobbies and other activities not relevant to your work. They may help you to build rapport with a recruiter, but the time and place for that is in an interview. When you're trying to get noticed by a single minded computer, these statements aren't helpful because they will never be used as key words for a position vacancy, and they take up scarce space on your resume.

The trick to writing a good electronic resume is to discipline yourself to include only those aspects of your qualifications that:

1. Can be described in key words the computer will recognize or the recruiter will notice, and

2. Provide additional detail that will differentiate your key words and, hence, you from the competition for a position vacancy.

If you can do that, you'll have a resume with genuine power and impact in today's high tech job market.

4

Sample Electronic Resumes— The Good, The Bad & The Ugly

The following resumes illustrate some of the most important principles involved in writing an effective electronic resume. The Comments box at the end of each resume critiques the resume and points out its key strengths and weaknesses. None of these resumes are perfect. Some are very good, others are not so good, and a few—well, let's just say they need a lot of work. Each is presented here solely to demonstrate the critical aspects of content and format in an electronic resume.

Jane Alexander
52 Wakefield Street
Reston, Virginia 06735

(703) 771-5342 (Res)   (703) 776-3345 (Bus)

Objective

Position in Life Care / Nursing Facility Management where educational background, practical experience and a commitment to provide dignitu and high quality service to residents will be utilized.

Education

UNIVERSITY OF CONNECTICUT, Bridgeport, CT
Master's Degree - Health Management (6/93)

PENNSYLVANIA STATE UNIVERSITY, University Park, PA
Bachelor of Science Degree - Business Administration (6/87)

NORTHERN VIRGINIA COMMUNITY COLLEGE, Sterling, VA
A.A.S. - Hotel Administratoin (6/77)

Experience

SUNRISE HOUSE, Reston, VA   6/87 - Present

Financial Services Administrator   5/91 - Present
- Manage financial services and accounting practices for 200-bed skilled nursing facility.
- Directly responsible for collections; successful in bringing collections debt down $100,000.
- Conduct mid-month collection analysis.
- Maintain accurate records of current financial status.
- Prepare individualized monthly billing, electronic billing to State of Virginia, daily and monthly census, and cash deposits.
- Prepare status reports on expired/discharged clients.
- Directly accountable for accounts receivable and Medicaid billing.
- Responsible for maintaining Medicare accounts (Parts A & B) as well as maintenance and collection of aged reports.
- Process co-insurance cases.

Operations Supervisor   6/87 - 5/91
- Managed and directed daily operations for facility serving 175-200 persons daily.
- Supervised, scheduled and evaluated staff of 30+.
- Responsibilities included purchasing, cost control, event planning, meal preparation, inventory control and quality assurance.
- Ensured State health and sanitation regulations were strictly adhered to.
- Coordinated policies and programs covering employee services and training.

FAIRFAX COMMUNITY COLEGE, Arlington, VA   1/91 - Present

Associate Professor
Teach course work which includes: Introduction to Hospice Industry, Front Office Operations (Personnel, Employee Relations, Accounting, Financial Reporting, Guest Relations, Security Management, Computer Analysis, and Management Philosophy).

Licensure

Licensed Nursing Home Administrator - VA #007731

ANALYSIS:

Strengths

- The detailed list of activities under each position includes many key words.

- The inclusion of the person's license and its number are very important key words. However, the date of the license should be noted.

Weaknesses

- The use of an Objective rather than a Key Word Summary forces the reviewer to search for the person's qualifications in the body of the resume.

- The Education section should not appear in front of the Experience section, unless the person is a recent school/college graduate. The most important qualification for a mid-career professional is her experience, so that section should appear first. The most important qualification for a recent school/college graduate is his/her up-to-date knowledge, so the Education section should appear first.

- The person's accomplishments (e.g., "bringing collections debt down $100,000") are buried in the text and hence difficult to find. That lack of visibility undermines their potential impact with reviewers.

- The use of italics will confuse a scanner and degrade the processing of the resume for a resume management system or computerized database.

- Misspelled words hurt the professional image of the individual and degrade the ability of the computer to identify her based on correctly spelled key words used by an employer.

James R. Johnston

Home: 412 331 8865   1707 Apple Avenue
Work: 412 772 4453   Philadelphia, Pennsylvania 15213

POSITION OBJECTIVE

Challenging Executive Management position in a progressive health care organization which seeks an individual with a diverse management background.

CAREER HISTORY

ST. LUKE'S HOSPITAL, VALLEY FORGE, PA   1990-Present

LOGISTIC DIRECTOR   Jan, 1990-Present

Responsible for the management of Purchasing, Storeroom, Shipping, Receiving and Supply Distribution for 300 bed primary care facility.

PITTSBURGH GENERAL HOSPITAL,
PITTSBURGH, PA   1986-1990

MANAGER OF PROCUREMENT   July, 1989-Jan, 1990
MANAGER OF LOGISTICS SERVICES   Feb, 1986-July, 1989

Responsible for the management of Purchasing, Inventory Control, Receiving and Distribution, Linen Contract and Transport Escort Service for 250 bed primary care facility.

THE HOSPITAL OF ST. JUDE, PITTSBURGH, PA   1981-1986

DIRECTOR OF TRANSPORTATION AND SUPPLIES   Aug, 1984-Feb, 1986
MANAGER OF ADMINISTRATIVE SERVICES   May, 1981-Aug, 1984

Responsible for the management of Supply Distribution, Mail Room, Linen Service, Transportation and Delivery Service and Housekeeping activity in the ancillary and clinic areas.

EDUCATION

THE INDIANA UNIVERSITY OF PENNSYLVANIA,
LAUREL HILLS, PA   MAY, 1981

Bachelor of Science Degree in Health Planning and Administration.

Resume of James R. Johnston
Page 2

ACCOMPLISHMENTS

- Implemented new prime vendor contracts, resulting in cost savings of $545,000 over three years.

- Reduced Purchasing staff by 10%, decreased the volume of purchase orders by 30%, while improving service delivery levels.

- Negotiated and implemented a modular office systems contract, resulting in cost savings of $123,000 in the first year.

- Oversaw implementation of Total Quality Management process in the Purchasing Department, improving productivity and raising performance standards for the staff.

AFFILIATIONS

- Member, Hospital Purchasing and Materials Management Association

ANALYSIS:

Strengths

- The individual's accomplishments are clearly set apart and can be easily identified.

- A relatively wide array of key words, particularly industry, quantitative and functional terms, appear in his list of accomplishments.

- His name has been included on the second page of his resume so it can be identified should the page become separated during scanning and processing.

Weaknesses

- The use of an Objective rather than a Key Word Summary forces the reviewer to search for the person's qualifications in the body of the resume.

- The chronological format of the resume provides very little information about and few key words for the skills and abilities exercised by the individual in each of his positions.

- The separation of Accomplishments from positions in the Experience section makes it impossible to determine where these achievements occurred and when, undermining their impact on the reviewer.

- The lack of any additional education or training since 1981 hurts the individual's credibility as an up-to-date professional with an expanding set of skills and knowledge.

- The use of responsibility statements rather than descriptions of what the individual can do and how well he did it in each position misses many of the key words necessary to match this person with a position vacancy.

JULIE M. BARTOW

7705 Georges Hall, P.O. Box 55   (903) 522 1963 (home)
Columbia, SC 27695-7487   (903) 753 8900 (office)

SUMMARY OF QUALIFICATIONS

Possess excellent supervisory skills; able to effectively lead, motivate, and inspire. Highly organized and energetic worker, able to manage many complex projects simultaneously. Committed to providing high quality programming and training, using adult teaming theory. Experienced in working with teams and individuals.

EDUCATION

University of South Carolina   Columbia, South Carolina
Master of Education in Training and Development with a Business Management minor, May, 1992; GPA: 3.34 4.0.
Bachelor of Arts in Psychology with Counseling minor, May, 1990.

COMPETENCIES

Administration Maintained budgets for training, supplies, recognition activities, programming for summer youth programs sponsored by the City of Charleston, SC. Designed and published biweekly newsletter. Managed a 22,000 square foot facility providing a full range of recreational activities.

Advising & Counseling Advised two student organizations involving approximately 4,000 male and female students. Counseled individual students with career and personal concerns as needed. Provided on call crisis management response for 6 residence halls and 4,000 students on a rotating basis .

Facilitation Facilitated training sessions and programs for staff and students on subjects such as: total quality management, communicating with others, motivation, creativity, enthusiasm and esprit de corps, leadership, goal setting, programming, publicity, and rape and sexual assault. Facilitated diversity programs in South Carolina High Schools, 1992 and 1993. Presented programs regularly at national, regional, and state conferences. Planned, coordinated, and facilitated staff retreat for 22 paraprofessional staff members. Instructed a two credit college course, entitled Introduction to Adolescent Counseling; topics included communication, values clarification, developmental theory, diversity, and crisis management.

Recruitment Recruited counselors for summer program. Reviewed and evaluated applications and resumes. Developed improved staff selection and placement process and procedures.

Supervision Selected, trained and supervised, and evaluated staff of 22 paraprofessionals. Selected, supervised, and trained 125 Camp Counselors, and 5 Counselors in Training.

Julie M. Bartow, Page 2

<u>Training</u> Trained staff of 22 paraprofessionals in recreational projects planning. Conducted needs assessment and evaluations of on-the-job training for 185 paraprofessional staff members. Developed curriculum and packaged training materials for staff training sessions, and student programs.

SELECTED PRESENTATIONS

"Total Quality Management: Buzz Word or Bonanza," South Carolina Society of Human Resources Conference 1992.
"Stretching Dollars for Student Programs," Staff Inservice Training, Fall 1993.

HONORS

South Carolina Society of Human Resources Conference 1992 Top Program Award.
City of Charleston Certificate of Appreciation, 1993.

ACTIVITIES

American Society of Training and Development (Member, 1992-present).
Society for Human Resource Management (Chapter Program Vice President, 1991-1992).
Intramural Advisory Board (Chairperson, 1991-1992, 1992-1993).

EMPLOYMENT

Housing and Residence Life, University of South Carolina, Columbia, South Carolina, Residence Director, May 1992-present.
City of Charleston Summer Program Coordinator, May 1992-August 1993.

REFERENCES Available upon request.

ANALYSIS:

Strengths

● The individual's Summary of Qualifications acts as a Key Word Summary, highlighting her principal knowledge, skills and abilities up front where they will be seen by overworked recruiters.

● The functional layout of her resume contains a large number of key words identifying her qualifications.

● The individual's name appears on the second page of her resume so that it can be identified should the page become separated during scanning and processing.

Weaknesses

● The use of a functional style format makes it difficult to determine in which position she demonstrated the knowledge, skills and abilities she describes.

● The use of a box around her resume will confuse a scanner, which will read the box's vertical lines as the letter "l".

● The use of small, 9 point typeface may make it difficult for a scanner to read her resume accurately.

● The use of underlining may make it difficult for a scanner to read/ process the resume accurately.

● The statement regarding her References is not necessary and a waste of space on the resume.

Brian L. Simpson
1901 Near Lake Road
Huntsville, AL 35818
(205) 762 4405

OBJECTIVE:

Hands-on manager with over10 years experience empowering high performance teams in software engineering analysis, supporting Space Lab and other NASA technology development programs. Seeking an opportunity in software engineering analysis that will expand my knowledge and foster career growth.

EDUCATION:

B.S. Computer Science minor in Mathematics, University of Alabama in Huntsville, 1977
M.S. System Engineering, Thomas E. Edison Institute of Technology, (In progress)

Additional Training
Object Oriented Design and Analysis
TBE Software Engineering Course
IBM's Trusted Software Development Training
Distributed Computing Design System (DCDS) Training
Requirements Tracer (RT) Training
Technical Writing Course

EMPLOYMENT HISTORY:

IBM Aerospace Engineering, Huntsville, AL March 1990 to present
Martin Marietta, Inc., Huntsville, AL May 1980 to February 1990
Hercules Space Systems, Montgomery, AL May 1977 to May 1980

COMPETENCIES:

CASE Tools Support
- Provided managerial assistance and user support
- Coordinated developer and integration efforts with the use of DCDS and RDD

Computer Services
- Established a classified link between the IBM Research Center in Huntsville and the NASA Test Facility at Cape Kennedy
- Managed both classified and unclassified processing; also provided computer administrative support such as computer purchase requisitions, software and hardware installation, resource allocations, and trouble shooting

Verification and Validation
- Performed requirements analysis, requirements traceability, application of Trusted Software Principles, and technical document reviews
- Reviewed and prepared documentation in accordance with Military Standards such as MU STD 2167A

System and Software Engineering Analysis
- Identified critical issues, measures of effectiveness and parameters for defining initial requirements and simulation support
- Interfaced with government customers

PROGRAMS SUPPORTED:
BKND Software, Next Generation Software Engineering Environment, VTXTS Flight System Simulator, Lance Missile System Test Bed, SDI Early Warning Radar Systems, and Space Lab

SECURITY CLEARANCE: SECRET, PRSDI, JCSINTEL
(Department of Defense)
U.S. Citizen

ANALYSIS:

Strengths

- The resume contains a large number of technical terms and jargon likely to be used as key words by recruiters seeking to fill very specialized positions.

- The resume lists special certifications, in this case the individual's security clearances for government work on classified projects.

- On-going education and training are included, signaling a person who has a growing level of expertise in his field and a commitment to advancing his professional knowledge.

Weaknesses

- The use of a functional style format makes it difficult to determine in which position the person demonstrated the knowledge, skills and abilities he describes.

- The use of an Objective rather than a Key Word Summary forces the reviewer to search for the person's qualifications in the body of the resume.

- The use of "soft" vocabulary (e.g., "hands-on," "empowering") takes up space on the resume without adding any key words that would be helpful in a computer-based search.

- The Education section should not appear in front of the Experience section, unless the person is a recent school/college graduate.

- The lack of identification on the second page of the resume could cause it to be lost were it separated from the first page during scanning and processing at the job bank.

- The use of italics will make it difficult for a scanner to read/process the resume accurately.

A Cut Above The Rest

In 1991, I founded and over the next five years, ran an electronic employment services company called Job Bank USA. A pioneer in the use of computerized resume databases, the company was eventually endorsed by over 400 professional, alumni and affinity groups across the country.

During its years of operations, tens of thousands of people sent their resumes to Job Bank USA. Those which follow are among the best we received. They have been carefully modified to protect the identity of the 1individuals whose credentials they describe. However, their key aspects—their format and content—remain largely unchanged. Consequently, they look and read much as they did when they were originally entered into the Job Bank USA computer.

These resumes stand out for one very important reason: they work. They have demonstrated both the capability and the power of an electronic resume. Indeed, these particular electronic resumes compiled very impressive records; each connected its owner with between five and twenty new employment opportunities!

As you will see, no single resume incorporates every one of the guidelines provided in this book. All of them, however, embody the key principles of an effective electronic resume design. As a result, these resumes accomplished two critical tasks which a conventional resume simply could not: first, they enabled the Job Bank USA computer to recognize and understand their owners' employment credentials and second, they matched those credentials with the qualifications that employers had specified for open jobs.

Undoubtedly, some of these matches were caused by other factors. A person's occupational field, location, salary requirement as well as the economy and time of year can and do have an impact. Nevertheless, these electronic resumes are useful models because they have a track record of success. They are not "make believe" resumes developed for a book, but actual working resumes that have met the test in the high tech job market of the 1990's. They made electronic connections between real people and real employment opportunities. Hence, while they are not perfect, they are a cut above the rest.

Each of the following resumes is presented on a single page for ease of reference. When produced at Job Bank USA and for employers using the recommended 10-12 point size, each resume was two pages in length.

JANE SIMEON
54 Old Oak Terrace
Phoenixville, Pennsylvania 42516
Home: (215) 555-4217

QUALIFICATIONS SUMMARY:

A skilled Human Resources professional with over ten years experience in personnel functions in both a bargaining and non-bargaining setting, with much of this experience centered on employee relations.

EMPLOYMENT HISTORY:

September 1991 to May 1994: Bluebell Building Products, Philadelphia, Pennsylvania
Personnel Manager—reported to the President/CEO of a manufacturing facility with approximately 400 employees. Involved in all corporate Human Resources related functions, including recruiting and hiring; compensation management; employee benefits; pension and insurance administration; labor/employee relations; contract administration; policy formulation; workers compensation administration; and training. Major emphasis placed on management and maintenance of employee benefit costs, improvement of labor relations with the bargaining unit, and enhancement of personnel systems to improve the efficiency and overall level of support to the organization.

Significant Accomplishments:
- Successfully participated in negotiating a four year labor contract meeting corporate objectives.
- Reduced annual cost for Worker's Compensation Insurance and Group Health Plan by over 20%.
- Designed and implemented policies for Family & Medical Leave, Americans with Disabilities Act, Drug & Alcohol Abuse, and Sexual Harassment.

January 1990 to September 1991: Pennsylvania State Employees Association Philadelphia, Pennsylvania
Labor Relations Representative—reported to the Director of Employment Services of a labor organization representing over 20,000 Pennsylvania state employees. Provided assistance to state employees with job-related matters. Investigated labor problems and established facts to support grievance preparation and represented employees through all steps of the grievance procedure. Negotiated with management of state agencies to facilitate dispute resolution and grievance settlement. Attended Association meetings to advise employees of changes in state law and personnel policies.

April 1984 to December 1989: York Industries, Inc., York, Pennsylvania
Human Resources Administrator—reported to the Human Resources Division Manager of a manufacturing facility with over 2,000 employees. Directed all recruiting and hiring of shop and office bargaining employees; administered labor contracts with respect to layoff, recall and job assignments; and conducted pre-retirement interviews explaining pension benefits. In addition, served in labor relations during periods of contract negotiation and also participated in the investigation and preparation of grievances for arbitration.

EDUCATION:
Gettysburg College, Gettysburg, PA, B.S.—Business Administration, Graduated Magna Cum Laude

PROFESSIONAL ORGANIZATIONS:
National and Local Chapter Member—Society for Human Resources Management (SHRM)
Tri-State Safety Council

JOHN ST. THOMAS, CPIM
42 Apple Pine Way
Monterey, California 90708
408-886-9828

KEYWORDS
Materials and Purchasing Management. Operations Management. JIT. MRP II. TQM. DRP. Focus Forecasting. Project Management. Cost Reduction. Cycle Time Reduction. EDI. Repetitive/Custom Job Shop. Lead Time Reduction. Vender Certification Program. Sourcing & Negotiating. Barcoding. Cycle Count Program. Inventory Control. Production Planning. Master Scheduling. P&L Responsibility. CPIM Certified. BA Business—1972. LLB Law—1977.

EXPERIENCE
Independent Consultant—Central California—October, 1991 to Present
Self-employed as contract consultant for small to medium sized companies in the areas of materials, purchasing, operations and distribution.
- Several successful JIT/TQM purchasing project implementations including vender certification programs, an EDI implementation, and re-engineering for buyer/planner concept.
- Member of project team which implemented multiple distribution center DRP/focus forecasting system with extensive re-engineering of all operational systems, procedures and processes.

Atlas Generating Corp.—Salinas, CA.
Operations Manager—1990 to September 1991
Directed manufacturing, purchasing, customer service, production and master scheduling, materials planning, shipping/receiving, and facilities. 1990 sales of $8 million.
- Planned, staffed, equipped, and established a new plant start-up facility which became operational within three months from inception.
- On time shipping record; sales bookings, production rate and shipments exceeded plan by 200%.
- Reduced material costs by 10%, manufacturing labor costs by 22%, and manufacturing cycle time from 6 weeks to 4 weeks on custom products.
- Implemented a LAN based MRP II integrated manufacturing information system which was fully operational within 6 months.
- Automated the contract/project material costing and bidding process to allow 24 hour bid response to proposals.

Atlas Solar Systems Corporation—Salinas, CA
Division Materials Manager—1986 to 1990
Directed production and inventory control, purchasing, materials planning, and shipping/receiving for a multiplant manufacturer of solar power generating equipment and industrial power drives. 1990 sales of $55 million.
- Reduced subassembly stock and WIP by 35%, raw materials stock by 15%, rework by 20%, shortages by 50%.
- Member of task force which implemented a manufacturing team-centered work force, facilitating implementation of JIT and TQM concepts and techniques.
- MRP II implementation task force member.
- Instrumental in developing and implementing kanban-type material pull system for repetitive product lines, eliminating the need for kit pulls, shop orders, and Subassembly Dept.

McDonnell Douglas Corporation—1976 to 1986, St. Louis, MO.
Inventory Control and Traffic Manager for a high-technology defense systems manufacturer. Worked in all inventory, stores, receiving and shipping functions.
- Sustained inventory record accuracy of 95%.

EDUCATION
- Degree in Law from Notre Dame University—1977
- Bachelor of Business Administration from Ohio State University—1972
- APICS Certification CPIM; Working on CIRM Certification
- Extensive seminars, courses, and workshops in Logistics, JIT, Operations/Manufacturing, TQM, Plant Management, CIM, etc.
- Computer software MRP II/DRP experience on FOURTH SHIFT, MAPICS, ASK MANMAN, MCBA, and ROTH DRP/Focus Forecasting system. PC experience with Word, WordPerfect, Lotus 1-2-3, Excel.

PROFESSIONAL AFFILIATIONS

American Production and Inventory Control Society
American Management Association
National Association of Purchasing Managers

PETER OWENS THAMES
5501 Brookfield Lane
Atlanta, Georgia 30301
Home (404) 755-1245
Office (404) 873-1123

SKILLS

Administration and Management Skills: program design; zero-based budgeting; contract negotiation; planning and providing logistical and administrative support/advocacy; meeting deadlines; recruiting and training staff; supervising and evaluating staff while promoting growth and increased productivity; cost effectiveness analysis; cost benefit analysis; presenting program accomplishments; advocating program needs; proposal writing; and writing succinct reports.

Communication Skills: human relations training; small group facilitator; interpersonal processing; teaching and evaluating communications skills; establishing decision-making models; technical writing; editing; writing for publication; newsletter production; computing/word processing; multimedia utilization; platform presentation expertise; fluent Spanish; read and understand Portuguese and basic French; cross-cultural communication; establishing internal communications systems; and knowledge of computer systems, networking, architecture, hardware, software, and services concepts.

Education Skills: training needs assessment; writing training objectives; design and implementation of evaluation procedures; instructional systems design and implementation; planning and implementing comprehensive educational assessments; conducting descriptive, quasi-experimental, and evaluative research; instructional materials design; writing curricula; teaching learning theory and adapting it to real-life situations; university teaching; and workshop planning, implementation, and evaluation.

EDUCATION

Ph.D., 1983, California State University; Major: Curriculum Development and Instruction; Minors: Human Resources Development and Non-traditional Training.

B.A., 1967, Michigan State University; Major: Latin American Studies/Spanish; Minor: International Economics.

Extensive Training at IBM (1/88—10/92—ranging from "Computer Hardware, Software, Systems, and Networking" to "Project Management.")

WORK EXPERIENCE

1988—Present, IBM CORPORATION
Instructional Designer, Sales Foundation Training   Andover, MA

Provided instruction and evaluation expertise to Software Services, Networking Systems, and Hardware instructors, as well as IBM's management; developed effective communication process with 25 technical experts throughout IBM; wrote book about IBM's service products, including text and end-of-chapter tests; provided Sales Foundation Training management with research/orientation about cost effectiveness analysis and cost benefit analysis.

1968—1987 (Intermittent), CALIFORNIA STATE UNIVERSITY
Various Positions & Responsibilities   Northridge, CA

Northridge Campus Faculty and Program Manager of Hispanic Leadership Program; Instructor in Communication Skills, Learning Theory, and Media Utilization; International Education Consultant; International Rehabilitation Research Assistant; Publications Research Assistant; International Development Research Assistant.

1986, COMPETITIVE SOLUTIONS CENTER, INC.
Director of Education   Northridge, CA

Developed curricula in entrepreneurship, personal power development, and fundamentals of management. Created and standardized instructional plan and trained instructors to use same.

1983—1986, EDITING SYSTEMS, INC.
Researcher/Writer/ Editor (Self-employed)   Northridge, CA

1975—1978, U.S. DEPARTMENT OF STATE
Taipei, Taiwan—**Nonformal Education Project Coordinator**

Managed and trained a team of 22 Chinese technicians (i.e., content experts, graphic artists, photographers, and administrative personnel) to develop and implement an instructional system (i.e., needs assessment, learning objectives, instructional strategies, implementation planning, and evaluation of results) appropriate for training adults in skills and knowledge they needed. Developed and implemented communication, cost control decision-making, as well as formative and summative evaluation models allowing expeditious fulfillment of project goals.

PETER M. WILEY
Box 712
Jamestown, Virginia 22309
(804) 469-0756

PROFILE

Human Resources Generalist with over ten years experience in positions of progressive technical responsibility, including recruiting, management development and training, employee relations, benefits, compensation, HRIS, Affirmative Action Plans, and outplacement.

PROFESSIONAL BACKGROUND

03/91 to Present   MANTECH CORPORATION—Norfolk, VA
Consultant—Training Specialist for a computer science/systems integration company.
- Coordinated of all employee training, including contracting with vendors to deliver on-site training
- Designed and delivered customized training as determined by needs analysis
- Organized MANTECH Chapter of Toastmaster's International
- Reduced cost of personal computer (PC) training by 33%
- Designed database system for recording employee training records as part of ISO 9001 compliance

12/88 to 02/91   DYNAMICS RESEARCH CORPORATION—Arlington, VA
Human Resources Generalist—Site manager for a 100 employee "satellite" office completing a Pennsylvania State contract to process health insurance claims.
- Expedited recruiting and expanded low cost sources of qualified applicants
- Received certification in Zenger-Miller's "Front Line Leadership"; coordinated and facilitated training modules
- Trained supervisors and managers in DRC's employee counseling and disciplinary policies
- Introduced and administered pre-employment drug testing program
- Organized and implemented outplacement programs including Job Fairs, resume books, and interviewing workshops

04/86 to 12/88   BDM CORPORATION—McLean, VA
Human Resources Recruiter for a highly technical, 800 employee corporate headquarters and research and development facility, working on an array of government contracts.
- Successfully recruited for engineers, computer scientists, programmers and managers due to the consolidation of two offices
- Wrote interviewing manual for supervisors and managers
- Supervised integrating 300 off-site personnel records into human resource information system (HRIS)

09/85 to 04/86   SCIENCE APPLICATIONS INTERNATIONAL CORP—McLean, VA
Human Resources Administrator for a research & development facility.
- Trained three HR Administrators in all phases of Human Resources
- Conducted monthly supervisory training programs
- Introduced and organized COBRA program and 401(K) Plan
- Initiated area salary survey
- Organized employee functions
- Facilitated employee group meetings

05/84 to 09/85   GOVERNMENT EMPLOYEES INSURANCE CO.— Fairfax, VA
Assistant Manager to the V.P. of Human Resources promoted from Human Resources Coordinator—for a major auto, life, home insurance company.
- Managed high-volume recruiting (220 employees the last year)
- Initiated and conducted the first in-house training programs using AMA Supervisory Programs as well as designed additional modules
- Wrote job descriptions for all office personnel
- Implemented new HRIS
- Reestablished and improved communications in Human Resources Department and offered an innovative method to deal with employee and management problems

EDUCATION
- Graduate work at George Mason University and Marymount Universities
- B.S. from James Madison University
- Certified Facilitator—Zenger-Miller's "Front Line Leadership"
- Additional Training in Human Resources at The American University and The George Washington University as well as numerous management seminars conducted by various employers.

PROFESSIONAL ORGANIZATIONS
American Society for Training & Development
Human Resources Exchange
Society for Human Resource Management
Toastmaster's International

ETHAN L. ALBRIGHT
P.O. Box 342 Ayer, Massachusetts 01667 (508) 876-9120

OBJECTIVE

-PROJECT TECHNICAL ENGINEER / INDUSTRIAL ENGINEER-
An experienced Project/ Industrial Engineer with strong manufacturing and project management background; considerable knowledge and experience in writing technical proposals; design, development and implementation of new manufacturing systems, assembly processes, and product line introductions.

QUALIFICATIONS

PROJECT MANAGEMENT
- Staff engineer responsible for all capital equipment planning and authorizations at company level, totaling over $50M.
- Management of financial overhead/direct expense budgets and manpower planning for Production Operations Group of 300 employees and $25 million annual spend plan.
- Staff lead of Production Operations Technical Proposal efforts for claims processing equipment contracts ranging from $50-$500 million.

INDUSTRIAL ENGINEERING
- Proficient with Industrial Engineering techniques in equipment and manpower capacity modeling, inventory control systems, process flow and time study analysis, profit improvement/cost reduction programs, plant layout and material handling systems, JIT techniques, cellular manufacturing, and production simulation modeling.
- A knowledge of good manufacturing practices; process specification control and standard operating procedures in a federally regulated clean room manufacturing environment.
- Proficient computer skills: Hardware—IBM compatibles, Apple Macintosh systems, Computer Aided Design workstations. Software-Word Perfect, AutoCad, CADAM, Lotus 123, Excel, ProMod, Simfactory, Witness, Harvard Graphics & Project Mgr.

SELECTED ACHIEVEMENTS

- Project Manager of 80,000 sq. ft. facility expansion and four major new equipment/product line introductions.
- Created manufacturing process plans on CAD systems for use by assembly personnel from build to print technical drawing and data package documentation.
- Directed Industrial Engineering design, layout and implementation efforts of automated material handling production line for mail sorting units.
- Implemented and headed plant cost reduction and profit improvement program resulting in savings of four million dollars annually.

EXPERIENCE

Staff Industrial/Manufacturing Engineer   3/90 - Present
Lockheed Corporation; Patent Systems Division   **Wilmington, Massachusetts**
Directed a group of five engineers supporting three unique product lines. Directed Company capital equipment planning, project management and authorizations. Administered overhead and direct expenses exceeding $12 million for Product Operations group. Head of Production Operations technical business project team preparing estimates on seven multi-million dollar programs. Coordinated technical documentation of proposed material and assembly process flow, manpower staffing, equipment capacity plans, and facility layouts.

Technical Services Engineer   4/88-3/90
Raytheon Corporation   **North Andover, Massachusetts**
Directed the validation of primary and secondary packaging equipment in the facility, including protocol writing, equipment and process validation and product performance qualification. Fact book was also included. Led introduction of new and existing processes transferred from other facilities into North Andover facility.

Materials Management Supervisor/Production Planner   6/79-3/88
Raytheon Corporation   **North Andover, Massachusetts**
Administered production control, planning systems/process transfers for facility producing over 300 products. Worked on manufacturing engineering projects for operations utilizing simulation and autocad software. Supervised warehousing, shipping, receiving and duplicating operations. Led team staff of 18. Developed systems for scheduling, forecasting, procedures control and performance appraisal and compensation.

EDUCATION

Bachelor of Science, Industrial Engineering, University of Massachusetts, May 1986.
Masters in Business Administration, Boston University, May 1992.

HONORS

1992 Honorary Inductee Society of Engineers, University of Massachusetts: honorary engineering society for outstanding industrial engineering accomplishments and leadership efforts since leaving the university.

JAMES P. LINLEY
41379 Emmitsburg Road
Dayton, Ohio 47621
(513) 722-8983

SUMMARY

Senior Instructional Technologist with expertise in the areas of needs analysis, consulting, problem solving, client negotiations and training design, development and implementation for educational, federal and corporate environments.

EXPERIENCE

Pacer Training Corporation   **Dayton, OH**
Senior Instructional Technologist   1/93—Present

- Design, develop and deliver software applications training and documentation.
- Conduct needs analysis and write course design documents.
- Manage development of task deliverables and consult with clients.
- Facilitate problem solving meetings and implement solutions.
- Develop and implement formatting standards for training materials.

Ameritech Information Systems   **Chicago, IL**
Instructional Technologist   1/92—1/93

- Developed and delivered training for 400 employees in multiple locations.
- Designed facilitator guides, participant manuals and job aids.
- Revamped product training; reduced course length and increased customer satisfaction.
- Assessed employee and client training needs and developed educational plans.
- Reviewed training sections of federal proposals and made recommendations.

Junior Instructional Technologist   6/90—1/92
- Analyzed evaluation data from training courses; compiled results and generated reports.
- Designed and implemented new evaluation instrument for in-house training.
- Coordinated training for 150 employees and negotiated vendor contracts.

EDUCATION

The American University   **Washington, DC**
M.A., Instructional Systems Design   December 1990

Pennsylvania State University   **University Park, PA**
B.S., English Education and Secondary Teaching   June 1985

Northern Virginia Community College   **Alexandria, VA**
A.A.S., Liberal Arts   December 1981

Dale Carnegie Leadership Institute   **Chicago, IL**
Certificate, Effective Leadership and Public Speaking   January 1991

OTHER SKILLS

Experienced in accomplishment-based curriculum development methodology; managing multiple priorities; executive presentations and customer relations.

Ameryl P. Brown
15 Singing Bird Lane
Minneapolis, MN 56997
(612) 446-9856

CAREER SUMMARY:

An accomplished Marketing and Sales Executive with increasing management responsibility across several industries from mid-size to Fortune 100 companies. I have a strong background in package good marketing, sales, promotions and financial services. A proven record of excellence in developing and implementing successful business strategies to maximize sales and profits. I have been widely recognized for outstanding leadership skills and involvement in civic, community and professional organizations.

EDUCATION:

Southern Michigan University, BS Economics/Business, 1970
University of Michigan, MBA, Marketing and Finance, 1976

PROFESSIONAL EXPERIENCE:

Metropolitan Life Insurance Company, Minneapolis, Minnesota

1991-Present, Division Director, Long Term Products Division
Launched the first new Group Insurance product in 15 years.
Formed a new marketing division to introduce Lawyers Long Term Care Insurance.
Developed unique strategic plan to launch this new product.
Generated first year sales that achieved 300% of plan

1989-1991, Division Director, Group Insurance
Supervised the marketing unit for the second largest product group in an insurance company with $22 billion GL and LTD insurance in-force.
Reversed negative plan termination trend and generated 5% growth.
Launched award winning and campaign and all star festival that increased displays 22% and customer trails and awareness.

Shasta Beverages, Inc., Atlanta, Georgia

1987-1987, Senior Product Manager, Alternative Beverages Division, Sales $109MM
Directed Shasta's largest non-traditional consumer product group.
Developed a corporate tie-in promotion for the 1986 Stanley Cup with NHL Properties and a dozen corporations.

1980-1986, Senior Product Manager and Product Manager, Iced Teas
Developed strategic expansion programs for iced teas. Achieved company's highest annual sales and market share in this category by:
    Creating first national consumer promotion
    Creating three linked commercials to increase interest, awareness and trial.
    Developing a modular display program that achieved the beverage's highest share of retail displays and inventory (23% and 45%).
    Growing market share 12% with greater ads and display support.
    Introducing decaffeinated version of iced teas, resulting in 15% sales increase.
    Cutting production cost by $4MM with IMA packaging project.
    Developing new packing graphics for entire product line.

NATIONAL CONTAINER CORPORATION, CHICAGO, ILLINOIS

1978-1980, Assistant Product Manager, Retail Packaging, Sales $55MM
Reversed declining sales trends and achieved 15% market share with new modular design introduction.
Conducted market analysis (SAM, A.C. Nielsen, Majers)
Developed and evaluated consumer and trade promotions.

1975-1977, Area Manager, Chicago
Supervised sales representatives, increased shipping package sales by 32% and display stand sales by 25% through monthly sales training seminars.
Secured National Container's first combined product introduction (valued at $300MM) at Stop ^ Shop Stores, the company's largest account.

1970-1975, Retail Sales Representative, Chicago
Consistently exceeded sales quota and won numerous sales contests.

PERSONAL:
University of Michigan, School of Business Board of Advisors, since 1991.
Selected "Outstanding Young Men of America," 1975 and 1982.
Honored for Outstanding Leadership and Contributions to the Business Community by University of Minnesota, 1990.

Albert J. Black
5216 Jayhawk Street
Seattle, Washington 98922
(206) 497-2094

CURRENT POSITION:
Project Manager for Curriculum Development with the Community Services and
Continuing Education Division, Seattle Community College, Seattle, Washington (August
1989 to present)

Duties include managing the Curriculum Development Project, estimate project costs,
monitor projects for quality and cost, supervise instructional designers, complete special
projects for Dean of Division and Department Directors. Hire instructional designers.

EXPERIENCE/SKILLS:
HEAD INSTRUCTIONAL DESIGNER with Professional Studies Institute, Seattle
Community College, Seattle, Washington: Supervise instructional designers and subject
matter experts and coordinate the design and development of instructional materials.
Conduct needs analyses and assessments; evaluate training and training materials.
Consult with internal and external clients including business, industry, government, and
educational institutions. Initiate and facilitate cross functional teams toward solving
identified needs and effecting change. Educate and develop internal staff and external
clients in the application of systematic instructional design. (August 1989 to July 1991)

TRAINING COORDINATOR with Microsoft, Inc. in Spokane, Washington: Managed
training function in facility of 2,000 employees. Coordinated development of facility-
wide training program, conducted needs assessments, evaluated program effectiveness,
and instructed management personnel in training methods and techniques. Performed
training specialist responsibilities. (April 1988 to July 1989)

TRAINING SPECIALIST (temporary) with Microsoft, Inc. (Became regular employee
07/01/85): Planned, produced, directed, and evaluated training programs and materials
using skills and knowledge in problem definition, needs assessment, writing, editing,
graphics, photographic, and videographic techniques; assigned and monitored training
and documentation of training; formulated training policies, using knowledge of
identified training needs, company production processes, and business systems; conferred
with and assisted supervisors and managers in delivering training.

ASSISTANT EDITOR with the Institute for Educational Studies, Washington State
University: Edited research manuscripts and supervised production; wrote articles for two
periodic newsletters; designed publications lists and catalogs. (1980 to 1985)

RESOURCE INFORMATION SPECIALIST/EDITOR with Department of Agricultural
Development, Washington State University: Wrote, edited, and supervised production of
a regional, monthly newsletter on agriculture and natural resource issues. This four-color,
offset-printed digest provided a missing news link for over 1,000 professional and citizen
groups in the Northwest. (1977 to 1980)
 MEMBER: American Society for Training and Development
         National Society for Performance and Instruction

EDUCATION:
- Master of Arts, Adult and Continuing Education, Cornell University. (1991)
- Course work in Media Technology Program, Spokane Community College. (1986 to
  1988)
- Course work in Commercial Art Program, Spokane Community College. (1980 to 1986)
- Bachelor of Science, Washington State University, Department of Agricultural
  Development. Curriculum included a cluster of courses in written, spoken, and visual
  communications. Other courses included land and water management, land economics
  and the like. (1977)

JAMES P. SIMMONS

8901 Abbott Street
Dallas, Texas 47711   (214) 446-8964

PROFESSIONAL SUMMARY

Analytical and detailed-oriented professional with over 16 years of experience in MIS, five years of materials management experience, seven years of experience in the marketing/sales of computer equipment, combined with extensive academic and training credentials.

AREAS OF EXPERTISE

Computer Operations   Materials Management
Systems Installation   Production Control Management
Account Management   Computer Security
Inventory Control   Budget Preparation
Forecasting & Scheduling

PROFESSIONAL HISTORY

E-SYSTEMS, INCORPORATED
Director, Management Information Systems, Dallas, Texas 1990-1994
Tasks and responsibilities included planning and installation of a MRP System, two Local Area Networks (LANs), an Electronic Data Interchange (EDI) and all software/hardware upgrades; establishment of computer security and disaster recovery procedures; technical staff supervision and software application analysis; software/hardware cost analysis; and contract negotiations with vendors and consulting for major strategic business unit.
- Reduced operating costs by 12% over a three-year period.
- Negotiated a five-year service agreement, saving $58,000 a year.
- Directed the conversion from MAI/Basic 4 to IBM AS/400 three months ahead of schedule, saving $29,000 in maintenance costs.

Director of Materials, Dallas, Texas 1990
Managed materials for the Software Systems Division, with responsibility for inventory levels, purchasing, production control, progress posting, forecasting, transportation and scheduling.
- Increased on-time customer shipments by 10%.
- Reduced inventory stocks by 14%.

IBM CORPORATION, Arlington, TX 1983-1990
Senior Account Representative
Sold software applications and hardware; managed accounts; forecasted sales; marketed computer solutions such as MRP Systems, Shop Floor Control, Bar Code Systems and CAD/CAM to manufacturers; and prepared contracts.
- Achieved over $22,000,000 in sales of goods and services.
- Company Achievement Award (1984).
- District Sales Champ (1983).

DELL COMPUTER CORPORATION, Austin, TX 1981-1983
Shop Floor Control Supervisor
Directed the master production schedule and shop scheduling; material movements in three shops; inventory control; and labor assignments in the Manufacturing Group.
- Increased the number of on-time customer shipments.

TEXAS INSTRUMENTS
Superintendent of Process Control, Dallas, TX 1978-1981
Managed the Master Production Schedule as well as material movements between five shops; progress posting; and shipping and manpower forecasts and utilization.
- Reduced shop lead times.
- Increased manpower productivity via improved movement of materials.

General Manager-Office Computer Operations, Dallas, TX 1973-1978
Managed computer security, system upgrades and maintenance across five computer facilities with 75 personnel; developed disaster recovery procedures; and negotiated contracts with vendors.
- Reduced overtime 50% by introducing a three-day work week of 36 hours for computer operators.

ACADEMIC & PROFESSIONAL CREDENTIALS

Bachelor of Business Administration
Major: Computer Science; Minor: Accounting
University of Texas; Arlington, Texas
American Production & Inventory Control Society (APICS)
CPIM Certification

5

15 Steps to an Absolutely Incredible Electronic Resume

The following 15 steps present a systematic, organized approach that will enable you to write your own absolutely incredible electronic resume. This process will not eliminate the thought, the energy or the time commitment required to develop any good resume, conventional or electronic. It does, however, give you the framework and direction you need to create an effective resume without wasting time, without a lot of frustration, and without the expense involved in having someone else write it for you. Follow this step-by-step process carefully, and you will produce your own electronic resume with the "right stuff"—the right format and content to plug you into today's high tech job market and connect you with the great job opportunities it offers.

Before you begin, however, take a moment to review the following important principles and procedures. They are the bedrock of the process, so you must understand and adhere to them for the process to work for you.

1. **Give your resume the attention it deserves.** Find a quiet room and enough time that you can get some concentrated work done. The step-wise process I've provided here will enable you to stop that effort at logical "break points," so that you can do something else (if you must) and then return to your work on your resume later.

2. **This is not a test.** In fact, I've included a reference note for you, in each of the steps. This note will direct you back to the appropriate place in the book where the step's particular aspect of resume writing was discussed. The references are there to help you understand the rationale and mechanics of how to write your resume and to assist you in completing it. So, don't rely on your memory; use the references as you work through the steps. You'll produce a better resume, as a result.

3. **You're doing something new and different.** You're developing a special kind of resume, an electronic resume. Don't mix the advice and counsel of relatives, friends, business associates or even professional resume writers, however well intentioned, in this process. Their background and frame of reference is almost certainly the conventional paper resume, and mixing that document with an electronic resume will yield a confusing and ineffective jumble of styles and techniques.

If you'll keep these guidelines in mind and follow the steps below, you'll have everything you need to develop one of the most advanced and powerful personal marketing documents available anywhere today—your own electronic resume.

Develop The Key Word Summary

Step 1
Determine the Selection Criteria for the Job You Want
Refer to pages 26 and 27

List below the critical qualifications for the specific position or category of positions you are seeking in your job search. Add to the list any other skills or experience that could enhance a person's performance on-the-job. These credentials are the selection criteria for the position you want. Your resume should be tightly focused on them. The following documents and resources will help you to identify these criteria: the position description for the new job, recruitment ads for the position or similar positions in your industry, the insights of other individuals who have held the position successfully in the past, headhunters or executive recruiters specializing in your field, and your own professional, technical or trade association.

_____   _____
_____   _____
_____   _____
_____   _____
_____   _____
_____   _____
_____   _____
_____   _____
_____   _____

Step 2
Identify the Key Words for Your Electronic Resume
Refer to pages 29 through 32

Identify up to 10 key words to describe each of your **ASSETS**. Record these words in the spaces provided in the first column below. The following documents and resources will help you to determine the nouns and phrases which best apply to you: any previous resumes that you've written, position descriptions for your current and/or past positions, performance evaluation reports from your current and/or past supervisors, the results of any skills or interest inventory assessment you've taken and the learning objectives for any education or training program you've attended in the past five years.

ABILITIES

Key Word	Synonym	Value
_____	_____	_____
_____	_____	_____
_____	_____	_____
_____	_____	_____
_____	_____	_____

SPECIAL AWARDS AND RECOGNITION

Key Words	Synonyms	Value
_____	_____	_____
_____	_____	_____
_____	_____	_____
_____	_____	_____
_____	_____	_____
_____	_____	_____
_____	_____	_____
_____	_____	_____
_____	_____	_____
_____	_____	_____

SPECIAL LICENSES AND CERTIFICATIONS

Key Words	Synonyms	Value
_____	_____	_____
_____	_____	_____
_____	_____	_____
_____	_____	_____
_____	_____	_____
_____	_____	_____
_____	_____	_____
_____	_____	_____
_____	_____	_____
_____	_____	_____

EXPERIENCE

Key Words	Synonyms	Value
_____	_____	_____
_____	_____	_____
_____	_____	_____
_____	_____	_____

_____   _____   _____
_____   _____   _____
_____   _____   _____
_____   _____   _____
_____   _____   _____
_____   _____   _____

TRAINING

Key Words   Synonyms   Value

_____   _____   _____
_____   _____   _____
_____   _____   _____
_____   _____   _____
_____   _____   _____
_____   _____   _____
_____   _____   _____
_____   _____   _____
_____   _____   _____

Using the spaces provided in the second column above, note the principal **SYNONYMS** in your field for as many of your key words as possible. These **SYNONYMS** are nouns or phrases that have the same meaning or a similar meaning to the key words you've listed for each **ASSET**. However, this step is not a dictionary exercise. In other words, you should **include only those synonyms that are used interchangeably in your field with the key words that describe your ASSETS.**

Step 3
Determine the Importance of Each Key Word in Your ASSETS
Refer to pages 26 through 30

Using the selection criteria you developed in Step 1, evaluate the importance of the key words in each of your **ASSETS** and rank order them. Assign a value of 10 to the most important and the value of 1 to the least important qualification you have among each of your **ASSETS.** The goal here is for you to designate the value an employer would use in evaluating prospective candidates for the job you want, rather than your personal judgment of its importance. Enter each asset's ranking in the space provided in the "Value" column above.

Step 4
Develop Your Key Word Summary
Refer to pages 30 through 32

The Key Word Summary is limited to 25 or 30 nouns or phrases that describe your most important **ASSETS** for the job you want. Therefore, using the rank ordering you assigned in Step 3, select the top five or six key words in each of your **ASSETS** and enter them in the spaces below. Remember, only the first letter of the first word in each entry is capitalized, and each entry is followed by a period.

_____.   _____.   _____.

_____.   _____.   _____.

_____.   _____.   _____.

_____.   _____.   _____.

_____.   _____.   _____.

_____.   _____.   _____.

_____.   _____.   _____.

_____.   _____.   _____.

_____.   _____.   _____.

Develop the Education Section
of Your Electronic Resume

Step 5
Document Your Employment History
Refer to pages 32 and 39

List all of your employers in reverse chronological order (i.e., the most recent first) and the dates of your employment. Each employer's name should be presented in all capital letters. State the month and year of each date as follows: 5/93—6/94.

Employer's Name   Dates of Employment

_____   _____

_____   _____

_____   _____

_____   _____

_____   _____

_____   _____

_____   _____

_____   _____

Step 6
Identify the Positions You Held While Working for Each Employer
Refer to pages 32 and 33

For each employer listed in Step 5 above, list the position or positions you held in reverse chronological order. Each position title should appear in initial capital letters (i.e., the first letter of all nouns is capitalized). Also state the month and year you held each position using the same format you used in Step 5.

Employer:_____   Dates:_____
Position(s):   Dates:

_____   _____

_____   _____

_____   _____

_____   _____

_____   _____

Employer:_____   Dates:_____
Position(s):   Dates:

_____   _____

_____   _____

_____   _____

_____ _____
_____ _____

Employer:_____ Dates:_____
Position(s):   Dates:

_____ _____
_____ _____
_____ _____
_____ _____
_____ _____

Employer:_____ Dates:_____
Position(s):   Dates:

_____ _____
_____ _____
_____ _____
_____ _____
_____ _____

Employer:_____ Dates:_____
Position(s):   Dates:

_____ _____
_____ _____
_____ _____
_____ _____

Employer:_____ Dates:_____
Position(s):   Dates:

_____ _____
_____ _____
_____ _____
_____ _____

Employer:_____   Dates:_____
Position(s):   Dates:

_____   _____
_____   _____
_____   _____
_____   _____
_____   _____

Employer:_____   Dates:_____
Position(s):   Dates:

_____   _____
_____   _____
_____   _____
_____   _____
_____   _____

Employer:_____   Dates:_____
Position(s):   Dates:

_____   _____
_____   _____
_____   _____
_____   _____

Employer:_____   Dates:_____
Position(s):   Dates:

_____   _____
_____   _____
_____   _____
_____   _____
_____   _____

Step 7
Identify the Knowledge, Skills & Abilities You Used On-the-Job
Refer to pages 33 through 37

For each of the positions that you identified in Step 6, use the key words you developed in Step 2 to list those qualifications and capabilities that you demonstrated in the position. These key words should identify all of the knowledge, skills and abilities you used to accomplish the tasks and activities for which you were responsible. You may include the same key word(s) in more than one position, but you should use all of the key words at least once. Wherever possible, use the synonyms of a key word, once the key word itself has been used in the Key Word Summary or for another position.

Employer:_____ Dates:_____
Position: _____ Dates: _____

Key Words:

_____. _____. _____.
_____. _____. _____.
_____. _____. _____.
_____. _____. _____.
_____. _____. _____.

Employer:_____ Dates:_____
Position: _____ Dates: _____

Key Words:

_____. _____. _____.
_____. _____. _____.
_____. _____. _____.
_____. _____. _____.
_____. _____. _____.

Employer:_____ Dates:_____
Position: _____ Dates: _____

Key Words:

_____. _____. _____.
_____. _____. _____.
_____. _____. _____.
_____. _____. _____.
_____. _____. _____.

Employer:_____   Dates:_____
Position: Dates:
_____   _____

Key Words:

_____. _____. _____.
_____. _____. _____.
_____. _____. _____.
_____. _____. _____.
_____. _____. _____.

Employer:_____   Dates:_____
Position: Dates:
_____   _____

Key Words:

_____. _____. _____.
_____. _____. _____.
_____. _____. _____.
_____. _____. _____.
_____. _____. _____.

Employer:_____   Dates:_____
Position: Dates:
_____   _____

Key Words:

_____. _____. _____.
_____. _____. _____.
_____. _____. _____.
_____. _____. _____.
_____. _____. _____.

Employer:_____   Dates:_____
Position: Dates:
_____   _____

Key Words:

_____. _____. _____.
_____. _____. _____.
_____. _____. _____.
_____. _____. _____.
_____. _____. _____.

Employer:_____ Dates:_____
Position:_____ Dates:

_____ _____

Key Words:

_____. _____. _____.
_____. _____. _____.
_____. _____. _____.
_____. _____. _____.
_____. _____. _____.

Employer:_____ Dates:_____
Position:_____ Dates:

_____ _____

Key Words:

_____. _____. _____.
_____. _____. _____.
_____. _____. _____.
_____. _____. _____.
_____. _____. _____.

Employer:_____ Dates:_____
Position:_____ Dates:

_____ _____

Key Words:

_____. _____. _____.
_____. _____. _____.
_____. _____. _____.
_____. _____. _____.
_____. _____. _____.

Employer:_____ Dates:_____
Position:_____ Dates:

_____ _____

Key Words:

_____. _____. _____.
_____. _____. _____.
_____. _____. _____.
_____. _____. _____.
_____. _____. _____.

Employer:_____   Dates:_____
Position: Dates:
_____   _____

Key Words:

_____. _____. _____.
_____. _____. _____.
_____. _____. _____.
_____. _____. _____.
_____. _____. _____.

Employer:_____   Dates:_____
Position: Dates:
_____   _____

Key Words:

_____. _____. _____.
_____. _____. _____.
_____. _____. _____.
_____. _____. _____.
_____. _____. _____.

Employer:_____   Dates:_____
Position: Dates:
_____   _____

Key Words:

_____. _____. _____.
_____. _____. _____.
_____. _____. _____.
_____. _____. _____.
_____. _____. _____.

Employer:_____   Dates:_____
Position: Dates:
_____   _____

Key Words:

_____. _____. _____.
_____. _____. _____.
_____. _____. _____.
_____. _____. _____.
_____. _____. _____.

Employer:_____ Dates:_____
Position: Dates:

_____ _____

Key Words:

_____. _____. _____.
_____. _____. _____.
_____. _____. _____.
_____. _____. _____.
_____. _____. _____.

Employer:_____ Dates:_____
Position: Dates:

_____ _____

Key Words:

_____. _____. _____.
_____. _____. _____.
_____. _____. _____.
_____. _____. _____.
_____. _____. _____.

Employer:_____ Dates:_____
Position: Dates:

_____ _____

Key Words:

_____. _____. _____.
_____. _____. _____.
_____. _____. _____.
_____. _____. _____.
_____. _____. _____.

Employer:_____ Dates:_____
Position: Dates:

_____ _____

Key Words:

_____. _____. _____.
_____. _____. _____.
_____. _____. _____.
_____. _____. _____.
_____. _____. _____.

Employer:_____   Dates:_____
Position: Dates:

_____   _____
Key Words:

_____. _____. _____.
_____. _____. _____.
_____. _____. _____.
_____. _____. _____.
_____. _____. _____.

Employer:_____   Dates:_____
Position: Dates:

_____   _____
Key Words:

_____. _____. _____.
_____. _____. _____.
_____. _____. _____.
_____. _____. _____.
_____. _____. _____.

Employer:_____   Dates:_____
Position: Dates:

_____   _____
Key Words:

_____. _____. _____.
_____. _____. _____.
_____. _____. _____.
_____. _____. _____.
_____. _____. _____.

Employer:_____   Dates:_____
Position: Dates:

_____   _____
Key Words:

_____. _____. _____.
_____. _____. _____.
_____. _____. _____.
_____. _____. _____.
_____. _____. _____.

Employer:_____   Dates:_____
Position: Dates:

_____   _____
Key Words:

_____. _____. _____.
_____. _____. _____.
_____. _____. _____.
_____. _____. _____.
_____. _____. _____.

Employer:_____   Dates:_____
Position: Dates:

_____   _____
Key Words:

_____. _____. _____.
_____. _____. _____.
_____. _____. _____.
_____. _____. _____.
_____. _____. _____.

Employer:_____   Dates:_____
Position: Dates:

_____   _____
Key Words:

_____. _____. _____.
_____. _____. _____.
_____. _____. _____.
_____. _____. _____.
_____. _____. _____.

Employer:_____   Dates:_____
Position: Dates:

_____   _____
Key Words:

_____. _____. _____.
_____. _____. _____.
_____. _____. _____.
_____. _____. _____.
_____. _____. _____.

Employer:_____   Dates:_____
Position: Dates:
_____
                                             _____
Key Words:

_____. _____. _____.
_____. _____. _____.
_____. _____. _____.
_____. _____. _____.
_____. _____. _____.

Employer:_____   Dates:_____
Position: Dates:
_____
                                             _____
Key Words:

_____. _____. _____.
_____. _____. _____.
_____. _____. _____.
_____. _____. _____.
_____. _____. _____.

Employer:_____   Dates:_____
Position: Dates:
_____
                                             _____
Key Words:

_____. _____. _____.
_____. _____. _____.
_____. _____. _____.
_____. _____. _____.
_____. _____. _____.

Employer:_____   Dates:_____
Position: Dates:
_____
                                             _____
Key Words:

_____. _____. _____.
_____. _____. _____.
_____. _____. _____.
_____. _____. _____.

Employer:_____   Dates:_____
Position: Dates:

_____   _____

Key Words:

_____.   _____.   _____.
_____.   _____.   _____.
_____.   _____.   _____.
_____.   _____.   _____.
_____.   _____.   _____.

Employer:_____   Dates:_____
Position: Dates:

_____   _____

Key Words:

_____.   _____.   _____.
_____.   _____.   _____.
_____.   _____.   _____.
_____.   _____.   _____.
_____.   _____.   _____.

Employer:_____   Dates:_____
Position: Dates:

_____   _____

Key Words:

_____.   _____.   _____.
_____.   _____.   _____.
_____.   _____.   _____.
_____.   _____.   _____.
_____.   _____.   _____.

Employer:_____   Dates:_____
Position: Dates:

_____   _____

Key Words:

_____.   _____.   _____.
_____.   _____.   _____.
_____.   _____.   _____.
_____.   _____.   _____.
_____.   _____.   _____.

Employer:_____   Dates:_____
Position: Dates:

_____   _____

Key Words:

_____. _____. _____.
_____. _____. _____.
_____. _____. _____.
_____. _____. _____.
_____. _____. _____.

Step 8
Document Your Experience in Each Position
Refer to pages 32 through 39

Using the key words for each position that you listed in Step 7, develop three-to-five sentences which describe what you did with those key words on-the-job. Do not use "responsibility sentences" (i.e., "I was responsible for this." "I was responsible for that."). Instead, write sentences that have three elements: the key word + a statement of what you did with them + some benefit achieved by those actions.

Employer:_____   Dates:_____
Position: Dates:

_____   _____

Key Word Sentences:

_____
_____
_____
_____
_____

Employer:_____   Dates:_____
Position: Dates:

_____   _____

Key Word Sentences:

_____
_____
_____

_____

_____

Employer:_____   Dates:_____
Position: Dates:

_____   _____

Key Word Sentences:

_____

_____

_____

_____

_____

Employer:_____   Dates:_____
Position: Dates:

_____   _____

Key Word Sentences:

_____

_____

_____

_____

_____

Employer:_____   Dates:_____
Position: Dates:

_____   _____

Key Word Sentences:

_____

_____

_____

_____

_____

Employer:_____   Dates:_____
Position: Dates:

_____   _____

Key Word Sentences:

_____

_____

_____

_____
_____

Employer:_____   Dates:_____
Position: Dates:
_____   _____
Key Word Sentences:

_____
_____
_____
_____
_____

Employer:_____   Dates:_____
Position: Dates:
_____   _____
Key Word Sentences:

_____
_____
_____
_____
_____

Employer:_____   Dates:_____
Position: Dates:
_____   _____
Key Word Sentences:

_____
_____
_____
_____
_____

Employer:_____   Dates:_____
Position: Dates:
_____   _____
Key Word Sentences:

_____
_____
_____

_____
_____

Employer:_____   Dates:_____
Position: Dates:
_____   _____

Key Word Sentences:

_____
_____
_____
_____
_____

Employer:_____   Dates:_____
Position: Dates:
_____   _____

Key Word Sentences:

_____
_____
_____
_____
_____

Employer:_____   Dates:_____
Position: Dates:
_____   _____

Key Word Sentences:

_____
_____
_____
_____
_____

Step 9
Document Your Accomplishments On-the-Job
Refer to pages 37 through 39

Identify one-to-three accomplishments that you achieved in each of the positions you've held. Wherever possible, these statements should include quantitative measures of the benefit or value of the accomplishment (e.g., "Improved sales 20% in just 6 months.").

Employer:_____   Dates:_____
Position: Dates:
_____   _____

Accomplishments:

_____
_____
_____
_____

Employer:_____   Dates:_____
Position: Dates:
_____   _____

Accomplishments:

_____
_____
_____
_____

Employer:_____   Dates:_____
Position: Dates:
_____   _____

Accomplishments:

_____
_____
_____
_____

Employer:_____   Dates:_____
Position: Dates:
_____   _____

Accomplishments:

_____
_____
_____
_____

Employer:_____   Dates:_____
Position: Dates:
_____   _____

Accomplishments:

_____
_____
_____
_____

Employer:_____   Dates:_____
Position: Dates:
_____   _____

Accomplishments:

_____
_____
_____
_____

Employer:_____   Dates:_____
Position: Dates:
_____   _____

Accomplishments:

_____
_____
_____
_____

Employer:_____   Dates:_____
Position: Dates:
_____   _____

Accomplishments:

_____
_____
_____
_____

Employer:_____   Dates:_____
Position: Dates:
_____   _____

Accomplishments:

_____

_____

_____

_____

Employer:_____   Dates:_____
Position: Dates:
_____   _____

Accomplishments:

_____

_____

_____

_____

Employer:_____   Dates:_____
Position: Dates:
_____   _____

Accomplishments:

_____

_____

_____

_____

Employer:_____   Dates:_____
Position: Dates:
_____   _____

Accomplishments:

_____

_____

_____

_____

Employer:_____   Dates:_____
Position: Dates:
_____   _____

Accomplishments:

_____

_____

_____

_____

Employer:_____   Dates:_____
Position: Dates:

_____   _____

Accomplishments:

_____

_____

_____

_____

Employer:_____   Dates:_____
Position: Dates:

_____   _____

Accomplishments:

_____

_____

_____

_____

Employer:_____   Dates:_____
Position: Dates:

_____   _____

Accomplishments:

_____

_____

_____

_____

Employer:_____   Dates:_____
Position: Dates:

_____   _____

Accomplishments:

_____

_____

_____

_____

Employer:_____   Dates:_____
Position: Dates:
_____   _____

Accomplishments:

_____

_____

_____

_____

Employer:_____   Dates:_____
Position: Dates:
_____   _____

Accomplishments:

_____

_____

_____

_____

Employer:_____   Dates:_____
Position: Dates:
_____   _____

Accomplishments:

_____

_____

_____

_____

Employer:_____   Dates:_____
Position: Dates:
_____   _____

Accomplishments:

_____

_____

_____

_____

Develop the Education Section of Your Electronic Resume

Step 10
Identify Your Formal Education
Refer to pages 39 through 42

List all of the formal degrees, certificates and/or diplomas you have received, in reverse chronological order. Next to each degree/certificate/diploma, identify the institution from which you received the degree/certificate/diploma and the date it was awarded. If you included the degree or certificate in your Key Word Summary, include it again here using a synonym or widely recognized abbreviation. Do **not**, however, use an acronym for your degree/certificate/diploma in the Education section.

Degree/Certificate/Diploma   Institution   Date

_____

_____

_____

_____

_____

_____

_____

Step 11
Document Your Continuing Education & Training
Refer to page 42 and 43

List any continuing education or training program you have attended in the last five years. Identify the subject or title of the course first, then the institution where you took it (or are taking it) and the date you completed it (or state "On-going" if you're still taking the course). Use key words from the list you developed in Step 2, wherever possible.

Course Title/Subject   Institution   Date

_____

_____

_____
_____
_____
_____
_____
_____
_____

Step 12
Document Your Licenses & Certifications
Refer to pages 42 and 43

List any licenses or formal certifications you have earned. Identify the formal name of the license, using key words from your list in Step 2, if possible; the institution or agency which awarded it; any identifying number or code which designates your particular license/certification or assigns it to you; and the date it was awarded or most recently renewed.

License/Certification   Agency/Organization   Identifying Number/Code   Date

_____
_____
_____
_____
_____
_____

Develop the Professional Affiliations and Awards Section of Your Electronic Resume

Step 13
Document Your Activities and Achievements in Your Professional or Trade Association
Refer to pages 43 through 45

List the professional, technical and trade associations or societies to which you belong. Identify any position you've held with these organizations and any major activity or task you've performed on its behalf (e.g., Conference Chairman, paper presentation) and the corresponding date for your involvement. Wherever possible, use key words from your list in Step 2.

Association/Society/Trade Organization   Position/Activity   Date

_____

_____

_____

_____

_____

_____

Step 14
Document Your Other Professional Activities & Accomplishments
Refer to pages 43 through 45

Identify any other activity or event in which you were involved that demonstrates your commitment to and on-going development in your field of expertise. List the organization or group which sponsored or supported your activity and then the activity itself, as well as the year in which it occurred.

Organization/Group   Activity/Event   Date

_____

_____

_____

_____

_____

Create Your Own Absolutely Incredible Electronic Resume

Step 15
Build Your Electronic Resume by Compiling
the Results of Steps 1-14 Above
Refer to pages 13 through 45

Compile the content of your occupational credentials into the format prescribed for an electronic resume. Then, input the document into a word processor and print it out with a laser printer or have it produced at a local copy shop. Use white paper and black ink to ensure its compatibility with the computer-based technology of job banks.

Your Name
Street Address
City/State
Contact Telephone

KEY WORD PREFACE:

_____. _____. _____.
_____. _____. _____.
_____. _____. _____.
_____. _____. _____.
_____. _____. _____.
_____. _____. _____.
_____. _____. _____.
_____. _____. _____.

EXPERIENCE:

MOST RECENT EMPLOYER:_____ Dates:_____
Most Recent Position:_____ Dates:_____
Key Word Sentences:

_____
_____
_____
_____

Accomplishments:

■
■
■

Previous Position:_____ Dates:_____
Key Word Sentences:

_____
_____
_____
_____

Accomplishments:

■

-
-

Previous Position:_____ Dates:_____

Key Word Sentences:

_____

_____

_____

_____

Accomplishments:

-
-
-

Previous Position:_____ Dates:_____

Key Word Sentences:

_____

_____

_____

_____

Accomplishments:

-
-
-

PREVIOUS EMPLOYER:_____ Dates:_____

Most Recent Position:_____ Dates:_____

Key Word Sentences:

_____

_____

_____

_____

Accomplishments:

-
-
-

Previous Position:_____   Dates:_____
Key Word Sentences:

_____

_____

_____

_____

Accomplishments:

■

■

■

Previous Position:_____   Dates:_____
Key Word Sentences:

_____

_____

_____

_____

Accomplishments:

■

■

■

Previous Position:_____   Dates:_____
Key Word Sentences:

_____

_____

_____

_____

Accomplishments:

■

■

■

PREVIOUS EMPLOYER:_____   Dates:_____
Most Recent Position:_____   Dates:_____

Key Word Sentences:

_____

_____

_____

_____

Accomplishments:

■

■

■

Previous Position:_____ Dates:_____
Key Word Sentences:

_____

_____

_____

_____

Accomplishments:

■

■

■

Previous Position:_____ Dates:_____
Key Word Sentences:

_____

_____

_____

_____

Accomplishments:

■

■

■

Previous Position:_____ Dates:_____
Key Word Sentences:

_____

_____

_____

_____

Accomplishments:

■

■

■

EDUCATION:

Degree/Certificate/Diploma   Institution   Date

_____

_____

_____

_____

Course Title/Subject   Institution   Date

_____

_____

_____

_____

License/Certification   Agency/Organization   Identifying Number/Code   Date

_____

_____

_____

_____

PROFESSIONAL AFFILIATIONS AND AWARDS:

Association/Society/Trade Organization   Position/Activity   Date

_____

_____

_____

_____

Organization/Group   Activity/Event   Date

_____

_____

_____

PART II

How to Write an Internet Resume

6

The Format of an Internet Resume

Unlike its paper and electronic cousins, the Internet resume is designed solely for its functionality. Its format, dictated by the realities of electronic information exchange, is neither eye-appealing nor memorable (except, perhaps, in an ugly duckling sort of way). However, the Internet resume makes up for its shortcomings in appearance with its extraordinary versatility and ease-of-use. Basically, you can send your Internet resume to any organization or person, located anywhere in the world in minutes or less, as long as they (and you) are connected to the Internet. Although you will still need a paper resume for your interviews, the Internet resume virtually eliminates the hard labor of a job search. Once you've written your Internet resume, you can say good-bye to copying resumes out on paper, folding and stuffing them into envelopes and carting them off to the post office to be delivered days or weeks later. In short, the Internet resume ain't pretty, but it gets the job done ... fast!

The format of an Internet resume is actually **a slimmed down version of your electronic resume**. All of the key elements that you included in your electronic resume also appear in your Internet resume and in the exact same order:

KEY WORD SUMMARY:
EXPERIENCE:
EDUCATION:
PROFESSIONAL AFFILIATIONS & AWARDS:

There are, however, very important differences between the two resumes. As noted previously, an Internet resume is one that has been developed in the common text language known as the American Standard Code for Information Interchange or ASCII. As a result, it loses most of the formatting conventions normally available in word processing software. It's not that an ASCII resume has no format, but that its format is genericized.

ASCII eliminates the embellishments that word processing includes to make the appearance of a document more pleasing to the human eye. As a consequence, it changes five specific aspects of your electronic resume's design:

1. The way key information is emphasized
2. The length of the lines of text and how lines are established
3. The way bullets or sub-categories of information are created
4. The way spacing is achieved between information and
5. The length of the Key Word Summary

These five features give the Internet resume its uniquely universal format, and it is that universality which enables it to move effectively from one computer to another, regardless of either machine's manufacturer, operating system or word processing application.

The Way Key Information Is Emphasized

In conventional paper resumes, emphasis is usually achieved by the use of capital letters, bold typeface, italics and underlining. In electronic resumes, the fickle nature of scanners narrows the tools for emphasis to capital letters and bold typeface. In Internet resumes, that choice is essentially eliminated. ASCII text will not recognize bold typeface, italics or underlining. As a result, if you want to emphasize information in your Internet resume, the only technique that will work is the use of all capital letters (which I'll call "all caps").

Since too many entries in all caps will diminish their impact, I recommend that you limit their use to the following three kinds of information:

1. YOUR NAME;

2. The principal section headings; i.e.,

KEY WORD SUMMARY
EXPERIENCE
EDUCATION
PROFESSIONAL AFFILIATIONS & AWARDS; and

3. The Names of Your Employers.

Using all caps with your name compensates for the limited formatting capabilities of ASCII text. Your name and contact information are usually emphasized in a resume by centering them on the first page. Unfortunately, however, centering is difficult to accomplish in the ASCII format, particularly the multiple lines required to present your contact information, so I recommend that you move your name and the contact information to the left margin of your resume and emphasize your name with capital letters. For example:

JAMES Q. SEEKER
1106 North Spring Field Drive
Allentown, Pennsylvania 66026
705-874-3302/jseeker@aol.com

Using all caps with the major sections of your resume and the names of your current and previous employers highlights key information that recruiters want to find quickly. It speeds their review process and makes it more accurate and effective for you. For example:

```
EXPERIENCE

JAMES RETAIL STORES      05/96-Present

Advertising Manager          05/96-08/97
Improved brand awareness by developing cooperative ad programs
with major product manufacturers. Developed new theme and
consistent look in all corporate advertising.
```

Finally, avoid the use of all caps within the body of your resume to emphasize any other points, no matter how important. While they may set off the information you are trying to convey, they will also undercut the impact of the other capitalized entries. However, you can and should continue to use "initial caps" (i.e., capitalizing the first letter in a word or phrase) in all terms where it is appropriate (e.g., position titles, degrees, institutional names).

The Length of the Lines of Text and How Lines Are Established

Many of the systems which read Internet messages and e-mail are limited to around 60 characters in width. If you use lines that are much longer than 60 characters or if you use the automatic "wrap around" feature in your word processing system to break your lines (which are also likely to be considerably longer than 60 characters), the text of your Internet resume will look disconnected and jumbled, making it very difficult to read.

Your best bet, therefore, is to limit the length of your lines to 60-65 characters, even though it creates a very "skinny" look to your resume, at least when it's viewed with a standard word processing application. In addition, you should break each line at the right margin with a hard carriage return, using the "Enter" key on your keyboard. While time-consuming to execute, this approach ensures that the lines break when and exactly where you want them to break in your resume. Further, in order to prevent the distracting look of uneven spacing at the left margin (see below), leave the single space between words or the two spaces between sentences **at the end of each line**, when inserting your breaks at the right margin. Since each space contains no character, its extension beyond the 60 character limit is not visible and hence does not detract from the appearance of your resume.

> Describe the knowledge, skills and abilities you currently use or demonstrated in this position in a three-to-five sentence paragraph. Use complete sentences but eliminate the subject "I," which is understood and becomes repetitive.

Remember, the goal is not to look like a paper resume but, instead, to ensure the accurate and undistorted transmission of your credentials on the Internet. Hence, when formatted correctly, an entry in the body of your Internet resume will look as follows:

> Describe the knowledge, skills and abilities you currently use or demonstrated in this position in a three-to-five sentence paragraph. Use complete sentences but eliminate the subject "I," which is understood and becomes repetitive.

The Way Bullets Are Created

Bullets are a key feature of your resume because they serve to highlight your accomplishments. ASCII text, however, does not recognize bullets. Therefore, while you must eliminate all bullet formatting from your Internet resume, you should replace it with a five-space indentation (created by hitting the space bar on your keyboard) followed by the plus sign ("+") and then another space. As illustrated below, this technique both sets your accomplishments off from the main text of your resume and distinguishes them with a special symbol. Although ASCII recognizes all of the characters and symbols which appear on your keyboard and some of these could also be used to highlight your accomplishments (e.g., "#" ">"), I think the plus sign is the most appropriate symbol for this purpose.

Describe the knowledge, skills and abilities you currently use or demonstrated in this position in a three-to-five sentence paragraph. Use complete sentences but eliminate the subject "I," which is understood and becomes repetitive.

+ List one-to-three accomplishments, setting each off by indenting five spaces with your space bar. Highlight each entry with a plus sign ("+") followed by one space and then your text.

The Way Spacing Is Achieved Between Information

Typically, we use spacing to give a document a more appealing look and thereby make it more enjoyable to read. Word processing applications incorporate a "tab" feature to enable you to create consistent intervals of space between information and to insert other spacing more easily into your documents. If you produced your electronic resume with a word processing application on your computer, you probably used tabs to set off some or all of the following kinds of information:

EXPERIENCE Section

- Dates of employment with various organizations
- Dates of employment in specific positions

EDUCATION Section

- Colleges, universities and other schools from which you have earned a degree or certificate
- Dates that the degrees and certificates were earned
- Licenses or certifications you have been awarded
- Dates that each license or certification was effective

PROFESSIONAL AFFILIATIONS AND AWARDS Section

- Memberships in professional associations
- Date that your membership began

- Leadership positions you've held in your professional/trade organization
- Dates you held these positions
- Titles of papers you have presented or published
- Dates the papers were presented or published

While such tabs are useful and effective, ASCII does not recognize them. Therefore, you should eliminate all tabs from your Internet resume and replace them with a consistent interval of spaces created by hitting your space bar. I recommend an interval of five (5) spaces because that is enough to set off one element of information from another, but is not so far apart that the resulting line length significantly exceeds the 60 character limit. For example:

MOST RECENT/CURRENT EMPLOYER   Dates of Employ

Title of Your Most Recent Position   Dates in that Position
Describe the knowledge, skills and abilities you currently use or
demonstrated in this position in a three-to-five sentence paragraph.
Use complete sentences but eliminate the subject "I," which is
understood and becomes repetitive.
    + List one-to-three accomplishments, setting each off by
indenting five spaces with your space bar. Highlight each entry
with a plus sign ("+") followed by one space and then your text.

EDUCATION:

Masters in Public Administration   Harvard University   1979

PROFESSIONAL AFFILIATIONS & AWARDS:

Authors Guild   Admitted as Member   1991

The Length of the Key Word Summary

Recruiters review Internet resumes much as they do those which arrive in the Human Resource Department on paper. The initial inspection is very brief and designed primarily to determine whether or not a person has the key attributes that would warrant a more in-depth assessment. When this review occurs on a computer, the more key information that is visible when the resume **first appears on the screen**, the more likely the recruiter is to see your qualifications.

Given the constraints under which today's recruiters operate, making them take the time and effort to scroll your resume down and read further into the text to evaluate your credentials is asking to be overlooked. Since the average screen size for most computers is about 15 lines deep, you should limit the lines required to display your name and contact information and your Key Word Summary to that length. For example,

---

JAMES Q. SEEKER
1106 North Spring Field Drive
Allentown, Pennsylvania 66026
705-874-3302/jseeker@aol.com

KEY WORD SUMMARY:

Human resource management and development. Ten years experience in health care industry. Compensation & benefits. Employee relations. Staffing. Union relations. EEO/AA. Succession planning. Vice President of Human Resources for 1,000 employee company. SPHR.

The Final Format

While adhering to the formatting guidelines described above requires considerable effort and attention to detail, you can get your computer to do much of the work for you. Simply make a copy of your electronic resume as a new file on your computer and then—depending on your word processing application—use the "save" or "save as" function to create a "text only" version (sometimes called a Rich Text Format or RTF) of the file. Using that document as your foundation, you can then begin to make the modifications described above and create your Internet resume. When you're done, the format should look similar to the example on page 113.

I understand that you might be a little uneasy using such a strange looking format unless you're sure that it actually works. So, I've given it a

YOUR NAME
Your Address
Your Telephone Number/E-Mail Address

KEY WORD SUMMARY:

This section contains the key words that a computer must see
in your resume to consider you a qualified candidate for a
specific position vacancy. When inserting your line breaks,
position them so that they follow the space between words and
the two spaces between sentences.

EXPERIENCE:

MOST RECENT/CURRENT EMPLOYER   Dates of Employ

Title of Your Most Recent Position   Dates in that Position
Describe the knowledge, skills and abilities you currently use or
demonstrated in this position in a three-to-five sentence paragraph.
Use complete sentences but eliminate the subject "I," which is
understood and becomes repetitive.
     + List one-to-three accomplishments, setting each off by
indenting five spaces with your space bar. Highlight each entry
with a plus sign ("+") followed by one space and then your text.

Title of Your Next Most Recent Position   Dates in that Position
with the Same Employer
Describe the knowledge, skills and abilities you demonstrated in
this position in a three-to-five sentence paragraph. Use complete
sentences but eliminate the subject "I," which is understood and
becomes repetitive.
     + List one-to-three accomplishments, setting each off by
indenting five spaces with your space bar. Highlight each entry
with a plus sign ("+") followed by one space and then your text.

NEXT MOST RECENT EMPLOYER   Dates of Employment

Title of Your Last Position With The Employer   Dates in Position
Repeat the format above.

Title of the Next Most Recent Position   Dates in that Position
Repeat the format above.

EDUCATION:

List your degrees, certificates, most important occupational
training and licenses in this section.

PROFESSIONAL AFFILIATIONS AND AWARDS:

List all of your professional activities, to include the professional
and trade organizations to which you belong.

test. I've taken this very format and pasted into an e-mail message which I then sent to myself over the Internet. When it arrived, I printed out the resume exactly as it appeared on my computer screen. I've reproduced the result on page 116. As you can see, the lines of the resume are intact and run together smoothly. The resume is easy to read and conveys its information clearly. That's what your Internet resume will look like when it's delivered to either an employer's home page or to an employment Web-site.

Subject: Test
   Date: Mon, 2 Mar 98 22:05:24 +0000
    From: Peter Weddle <pdweddle@worldnet.att.net>
      To: pdweddle@worldnet.att.net

```
YOUR NAME
Your Address
Your Telephone Number/E-Mail Address

KEY WORD SUMMARY:

This section contains the key words that a computer must see
in your resume to consider you a qualified candidate for a
specific position vacancy.  When inserting your line breaks,
position them so that they follow the space between words and
the two spaces between sentences.

EXPERIENCE:

MOST RECENT/CURRENT EMPLOYER        Dates of Employ

Title of Your Most Recent Position      Dates in that Position
Describe the knowledge, skills and abilities you currently use or
demonstrated in this position in a three-to-five sentence paragraph.
Use complete sentences but eliminate the subject "I," which is
understood and becomes repetitive.
     + List one-to-three accomplishments, setting each off by
indenting five spaces with your space bar.  Highlight each entry
with a plus sign ("+") followed by one space and then your text.

Title of Your Next Most Recent Position      Dates in that Position
with the Same Employer
Describe the knowledge, skills and abilities you demonstrated in
this position in a three-to-five sentence paragraph.  Use complete
sentences but eliminate the subject "I," which is understood and
becomes repetitive.
     + List one-to-three accomplishments, setting each off by
indenting five spaces with your space bar.  Highlight each entry
with a plus sign ("+") followed by one space and then your text.

NEXT MOST RECENT EMPLOYER      Dates of Employment

Title of Your Last Position With The Employer      Dates in Position
Repeat the format above.

Title of the Next Most Recent Position      Dates in that Position
Repeat the format above.

EDUCATION:

List your degrees, certificates, most important occupational
training and licenses in this section.

PROFESSIONAL AFFILIATIONS & AWARDS:

List all of your professional activities, to include the professional
and trade organizations to which you belong.
```

116

7

The Content of an Internet Resume

As with its format, the content of an Internet resume is derived from the content you developed for your electronic resume. Unlike the formatting process, however, your modifications will involve just three steps:

1. Reviewing and updating
2. Text cleansing and
3. Spellchecking.

Reviewing and Updating

A good resume, whether it is designed to be produced on paper, to be processed electronically or to be transmitted over the Internet, is a living document. Hence, this step gives you an important opportunity to make sure that the content of your resume expresses your credentials with as much clarity and impact as you can muster.

As with your electronic resume, the content of your Internet resume is only as good as the key words you have used to describe your qualifications. Therefore, make sure that you check over your ASSETS—your Abilities, Special Awards and Recognition, Special Licenses and Certifications, Experience, Training and Synonyms—to ensure that nothing has been left out in your inventory of credentials.

In addition, review your Key Word Summary to ensure that it is up-to-date and leads with your strengths. Remember, it should include the most important twenty-to-thirty skills and experience areas that you can offer to an employer, expressed in nouns and short phrases. Make sure, however, that you do not use more than 15 lines to state your name, contact information and the Key Word Summary. Otherwise, you will exceed the viewing space of most computer screens, forcing the reader to scroll your resume and limiting the impact of your Key Word Summary.

Finally, check your entries under Experience, Education and Professional Affiliations and Awards to make sure that they are current and accurate. Every entry should satisfy the two tests of good content in a high tech resume. They must describe:

1. What You Can Do, and

2. How Well You Can Do It.

If your review identifies necessary improvements or updates, make those changes right away. Be sure to include your modifications in **both** your electronic resume and your Internet resume.

Text Cleansing

As noted earlier, ASCII will recognize only those characters, numbers and symbols which appear on your keyboard. Hence, you should carefully check the text of your electronic resume and cleanse it of any nonfunctional figures. You will want to eliminate or replace all of the following:

1. Symbols

    - Greek symbols, such as Φ, Θ and , Ω
    - Mathematical symbols, such as $\pm$, ∞ and $\therefore$ (Using the plus sign ["+"] to set off your accomplishments is acceptable because it appears on your keyboard.), and
    - Business symbols, such as ©, ® and ™.

2. "Smart quotes" which are sometimes inserted when you use the quotation mark (") in your word processing application.

3. Hyphenated line breaks which are automatically inserted in most current versions of word processing applications. Given the difficulty of determining precisely where line breaks will occur when ASCII text appears on different browsers and e-mail readers, it is best to avoid hyphenated line breaks. However, you can and should use hyphens in those words and phrases where they are integral to their expression and grammatically correct (e.g., German-American, twenty-two, left-handed).

Spellchecking

Once you've reviewed and cleansed the content for your Internet resume, you should ensure that it is "picture perfect" for transmission to an employer or recruiter. Unfortunately, once you have pasted your Internet resume into the input form of an employment Web-site or into an e-mail message you are sending to an employer, it is too late to use the computer to help you proofread what you have written. Therefore, to prevent potentially embarrassing errors from creeping into your resume, the best practice is to:

1. Use the spellcheck function of your word processing application while you are developing your content; and then

2. Carefully proofread what you have written to confirm that all errors of grammar, syntax, logic and clarity have been caught and eliminated, when the resume is finished.

Once you've completed these steps, your content is ready for transmission on the Internet. The following chapter presents a number of resumes which illustrate the correct format and content of an Internet resume.

8

Sample Internet Resumes

The following resumes illustrate the format and content of an Internet resume for:

1. A senior level manager
2. A person with 10+ years of experience in the workforce and
3. A person seeking an entry level job after graduation from college.

As with the illustrative electronic resumes presented earlier, these resumes are not perfect. They do, however, incorporate many of the most important elements of an effective Internet resume.

Sample Internet Resume For a Senior Manager

LARRY B. OLSEN
1433 Fairfax Avenue
McLean, Virginia 22102
(703) 587-3260/larryo@aol.com

KEY WORD SUMMARY:

Start-ups. Small business. Entrepreneur. Leader. General
management. Chief Executive Officer. Consulting. Human
resource management. Technical services. High technology
design and development. Systems analysis. Education and
training. Private sector consulting and government contracting.
Rapid growth. Profitability.

EXPERIENCE:

CAPITAL RESEARCH CORPORATION

Chief Executive Officer   1994-Present
Direct all operations of this international consulting firm,
operating in 10 countries and performing projects for
numerous Departments and Agencies of the U.S. Federal
Government as well as private sector clients and international
entities such as the World Health Organization. Provide
technical services in human resource management, advanced
technology system design and development, education and
training.
    +   Within two years, tripled the Company's profits, and
doubled its backlog of contract business to over $45 million.
    +   Directed the Company's successful expansion into
private sector consulting, expanding its base of customers
and its resilience to business downturns.

Division Vice President   1988-1994
Managed a strategic business unit which generated over
$10 million in revenue annually. Directed all aspects of
division operation, including staffing, sales and marketing,
project management, quality control and customer relations.
    +   Directed the proposal and bid team which won the
largest contract award in the Company's history.

+ Achieved continuous revenue and earnings growth over six year period.

ORION SYSTEMS, INC.   1986-1988

Senior Project Manager
Managed large scale technical projects for clients in the U.S. Federal Government designed to improve individual and team performance in complex organizations. Conceived the marketing strategy, directed the bid and proposal effort, and oversaw technical performance, budget and quality assurance for three competitively awarded projects.

+ Marketing success led to the Company's selection by the press as one of the Fast 50, the fifty fastest growing firms in the Mid-Atlantic region.

+ All projects were completed on time and within budget, earning the Company a performance bonus from the client.

DYNAMIC RESEARCH CORPORATION   1979-1986

Project Manager   1984-1986
Directed all aspects of a major systems analysis and research project with the U.S. Department of the Army. Planned and assigned all technical tasks and oversaw their completion according to plan and budget. Presented project reviews to the client and drafted the final technical report.

+ Client cited report in testimony before the U.S. Congress.

Team Leader   1979-1984
Managed a three-person, multi-disciplinary team conducting research on predictive models for human resource requirements generated by alternative system designs for advanced technology systems. Communicated with the client on a regular basis and wrote a major section of the final project report.

+ Took over demoralized team and upgraded performance in time to meet its deadline for a project technical report.

EDUCATION:

M.B.A. Harvard University   1979
M.S.   George Washington University   1978
B.S. Wake Forest   1976

Sample Internet Resume For a Person With 10+ Years of Work Experience

JASON F. SNABEL
Sound Beach Apartments
Apartment 1701
Stamford, CT 06901
(203) 742-8871

KEY WORD PREFACE:

Database and resume management systems. Document and collections management. Web-site development. Internet. Database Management Systems. Microsoft and Netscape browsers. HTML. Customer service. Marketing. Process improvement. Productivity improvement.

EXPERIENCE

NEW YORK PUBLIC LIBRARY   6/96-Present

Staff Bibliographer
Handle new text acquisitions and various cataloguing duties throughout library. Use Internet, e-mail, and computerized library database and cataloging system to review and up-date contents of collections. Support Chief Bibliographer in major project to organize and stream-line text acquisitions process.
  + Process improvements cut re-order requirements by 15%.
  + Awarded merit salary increase in first annual review.

CAREERS ONLINE NETWORK   5/93-5/96

Database Administrator
Maintained database of over 25,000 resumes, while servicing all customer needs and inquiries. Worked with software and system vendors to continually update and improve database technology and operation. In constant contact with customers and client organizations to facilitate database performance improvement.
  + Developed new customer order form which improved data entry and generated positive customer feedback.

+ Cut system down time by over 10%, improving productivity of operations.

UNITED STATES DEPARTMENT OF JUSTICE   05/89-09/93
Expert Witness Unit

Database Technician
Selected from nationwide applicant pool to work in service unit within the Environment and Natural Resource Division of the Department of Justice. Developed and maintained database of resumes of expert witnesses. Worked with specialized unit to streamline database for use by Federal attorneys preparing for litigation.

+ Designed and taught course on database use for attorneys.

TRAVELERS INSURANCE COMPANY   06/86-05/89

System Support Associate
Worked on database team performing system upgrade and problem resolution support to nationwide cadre of insurance agents. Helped improve the accuracy of data input by designing self-explanatory on-screen prompts and usefulness of output products by revising format for reports. Manned Help Desk and provided on-call assistance to field users.

+ Consistently received superior performance ratings from supervisor.

EDUCATION

Bachelor of Arts   Tufts University   1986
DBMS Certificate   Fairfax Community College   1988

On-the-job training in Web-site construction, HTML coding language, Netscape and Microsoft browsers, and various search engines.

PROFESSIONAL AFFILIATIONS AND AWARDS

National Association of Database
Administrators   Member   1990

Sample Internet Resume For Person
Seeking an Entry-Level Position

LINDA P. HAIGI
1105 Sweet Hall
Manhattanville College
Purchase, New York 10477
(212) 778-3456/lhiagi@emerald.mnhtnvl.edu

KEY WORD PREFACE:

Systems engineering. Bachelor of Science degree.
Experience with power engineering consulting firm and
municipal utility. Research in human-machine interface
of maintenance subsystem designs and procedures.
Managed budget, staff and inventory for small business.

EDUCATION:

Bachelor of Science   Manhattanville College   1998
Major: Systems Engineering   Minor: Spanish

EXPERIENCE:

COLLINS & WAGONNER
CONSULTING ENGINEERS   Summer, 1997

Project Team Member
Contributed to an interdisciplinary team under contract with
a major shipbuilder to develop improved plans for maintenance
subsystems of shipboard power plants. Conducted research in
foreign literature on alternative approaches used in vessel power
plant designs. Wrote reports and conducted briefings on findings.
   +   Completed research project planned for three months in
six weeks.
   +   Expanded project to include literature reviews in Spanish
language engineering reports from Central and South America.

FAIRFAX COUNTY
ENGINEERING DEPARTMENT   Summer, 1996

Engineering Intern
Worked with the various power generating facilities in large
suburban county to ensure maximum operating efficiency and
power output. Assisted in troubleshooting maintenance problems
and in developing alternative procedures for repairing aging
equipment installed in various county facilities.

    +   Helped maintenance crews restore power to county
facilities after lightening strike damage from major summer
storm.

    +   Documented repair work-arounds so that they could be
standardized and replicated in the future.

CAMPUS EXPRESS COLLEGE STORE

Store Manager   School Year 1995-96
Cashier   School Years 1992-1995
Helped finance college education by working all four years at
school's on-campus convenience store. Advanced from junior
clerk on night shift to one of two student store managers.
Oversaw staffing of all day shifts, daily receipts reconciliation,
customer service efforts and inventory management.

    +   Increased store revenues by 25% in one year as store
manager.

    +   Reduced pilferage by 10% by improving training of student
staff.

PROFESSIONAL AFFILIATIONS AND AWARDS:

National Society of Professional
Engineers (NSPE)   Member, Student Chapter   1994-98
American Business
Women's Association (ABWA)   Associate Member   1997-98

9

10 Steps to an Absolutely Incredible Internet Resume

As noted in previous chapters, there are important differences between electronic and Internet resumes. There are also key similarities—in both content and format—and these common aspects give you three big advantages:

1. **You don't have to write two entirely different resumes**. Your electronic resume can serve as the foundation for your Internet resume. You'll need to make several critical modifications, but you won't have to start writing your Internet resume from scratch. In fact, the first step in the following 10-step process for writing your Internet resume involves reviewing and updating the content and format of your completed electronic resume. If you don't want to develop and use an electronic resume, you will still have to create the content and format for your Internet resume, and the best guide for doing that is the 15-step process provided for the development of your electronic resume.

2. **The information that you provide in your two resumes will be consistent**. With both resumes sharing a common baseline, there is much less room for confusing and potentially embarrassing

differences in the information you provide. That's important because employers often use multiple sources when searching for candidates and may receive two copies of your resume—one that you send in directly for processing in the organization's resume management system and the other which the employer obtains from an on-line employment Web-site. The employer's receipt of two resumes is not a problem, but disagreements in the information that appears on each can raise questions and, worse, stimulate doubts.

3. **You will have the tools to conduct a job search on multiple fronts**. After completing the resume, you will have:

   ■ An electronic resume that works with both the resume manage-ment systems used by employers and the computerized candi-date databases maintained by employment agencies and search firms and those employment Web-sites which process paper resumes into their on-line resume databases. That same resume will also stand you in good stead when it is reviewed by recruiters and others in employers' Human Resource Depart-ment.

   ■ An Internet resume that you can both transmit via e-mail over the Internet to employers and paste into the on-line enrollment forms used by a growing number of employment Web-sites to build their resume databases.

The 10-Step Process For Developing Your Internet Resume

Each step below is organized into a series of tasks you must execute to develop your Internet resume. The tasks are presented in checklist form so that you can keep track of your progress. For best results, perform the tasks and complete the steps in the order they are presented. As with the development of your electronic resume, this process is not a test, so don't rely on your memory if you have a question. Use the designated reference page(s) to refer back to the appropriate section in Chapters 6-7.

Step 1
Review and Update Your Electronic Resume
Refer to Pages 72 and 73

_____ Review and update your ASSETS

_____ Ensure that all entries state "what you can do" and "how well you can do it"

_____ Review and, if necessary, update your Key Word Summary

Step 2
Spellcheck the Resume
Refer to Pages 119 and 120

_____ Use the spellcheck function on your word processor to confirm the spelling of all words appearing in your resume

_____ Confirm the accuracy of all technical terms and jargon which appear in your resume but are not listed in your spellchecker

Step 3
Re-Format Your Electronic Resume into ACSII Text
Refer to Pages 114 and 115

_____ Use the "save" or "save as" function in your word processor to create an ASCII text (.txt) version of your resume

_____ Delete all word processing symbols (e.g., those indicating the placement of bullets) from the text

Step 4
Change the Way Information is Emphasized
Refer to Pages 108 through 110

_____ Re-format your name into all capital letters and ensure that it and your contact information are left justified

_____ Ensure that the following entries appear in all capital letters

- KEY WORD SUMMARY
- EXPERIENCE

- EDUCATION
- PROFESSIONAL AFFILIATIONS AND AWARDS and
- The NAMES of all employers for which you have worked

Step 5
Change the Length of the Lines of Text and How
Lines Are Established
Refer to Pages 110 and 111

_____ Break all lines in your resume at 60-65 characters, using a hard carriage return (When making your breaks, include the space between words and the spaces between sentences at the end of the line where the break occurs, not at the beginning of the next line.)

_____ Check the line length for entries of employers' names and position titles and for entries in the EDUCATION and PRO-FESSIONAL AFFILIATIONS AND AWARDS sections to ensure that they do not exceed the 60-65 character limit. If necessary, make special breaks as shown below:

```
COLLINS & WAGONNER
CONSULTING ENGINEERS                    Summer, 1997


American Business
Women's Association (ABWA)  Associate Member    1997-98
```

Step 6
Change the Way Bullets Are Created
Refer to Pages 111 and 112

_____ Indent all bulleted items five spaces, using the space bar on your keyboard

_____ Insert a plus sign ("+") and a space at the beginning of each bulleted item in place of the bullet, as illustrated below:

```
 + Increased store revenues by 25% in one year as store
manager.
```

Note that the second and subsequent lines of all bulleted items are **not** indented.

Step 7
Change the Way Spacing is Achieved Between Information
Refer to Pages 112 and 113

_____ Check your resume to be sure that all tab formatting was eliminated when the resume was converted into ASCII text

_____ Insert five spaces between the names of all employers you have listed and the dates of your employment with them

_____ Insert five spaces between the titles of all positions you have listed and the dates you held them

_____ Insert five spaces between all educational degrees and certificates you have listed and the colleges, universities and other schools which awarded them and between the colleges, universities and other schools you have listed and the dates the degrees and certificates were awarded

_____ Insert five spaces between all professional associations and publications you have listed and the membership, leadership position, paper title or other activity you have cited and between the membership, leadership position, paper title or other activity you listed and the date it occurred

Step 8
Check The Length of Your Key Word Summary
Refer to Pages 113 and 114

_____ Ensure that your name, contact information and Key Word Summary do not exceed a total of 15 lines, top-to-bottom

Step 9
Cleanse the Text of Non-Functional Characters
Refer to Pages 119 and 120

_____ Eliminate or replace all Greek, mathematical (except those appearing on your keyboard) and business symbols from the text of your resume

_____ Eliminate all "smart quotes" from the text of your resume

_____ Eliminate the hyphen from all hyphenated words appearing at line breaks in your resume (Leave all hyphens for compound words which, by convention, appear with hyphens; e.g., twenty-six.)

Step 10
Test Your Internet Resume

_____ Test your Internet resume by sending it to yourself via e-mail. If you have any questions about that process, follow the steps below:

A. Highlight the entire resume by holding down the left hand button on your mouse

B. Hold down the "control" key (sometimes designated "Ctrl") and press the letter "c" key

C. Close your word processing application; if a dialog box appears and asks if you want to save the text on your notepad, click "yes"

D. Open your connection to the Internet

E. Once you are on-line, open your e-mail program and then your file for sending a new message

F. Enter your own e-mail address in the "To" box and tab down to the text area of the message format

G. To paste your resume into the e-mail message, hold down the "control" key and press the letter "v" key

H. Scroll back up to the top of your message and use your mouse to click on the "send" button.

Depending on Internet usage at the time, it could take anywhere from seconds to hours or more for your resume to arrive. Once it does, open the message and print it out. Review the text carefully and make any necessary adjustments to ensure that both its content and format are correct.

PART III

How to Achieve Absolutely Incredible Results With Your Electronic and Internet Resume

10

The New World of Work

The Internet. The Information Superhighway. The technological bridge over political boundaries, geographical barriers, poverty and our cultural, ethic and religious differences. The worldwide network of computers that transforms us all into citizens in a global village.

The Internet is perhaps the most talked about topic of the 1990's. Yet, in 1994, just 3.1 million Americans were on-line and using the Internet for business or pleasure. That doesn't seem like much of a bandwagon—just over 1% of the American population—for something that was almost endlessly on the cover of every major magazine and newspaper, the subject of countless radio and television programs and the cause of ponderous pronouncements by high Government officials and business pundits.

So, why all the furor? Simple. From that modest beginning, the Internet has burst to life all over the country and around the world as a resource for communications and commerce, distance learning and dispersed staffing, business transactions and news, research and entertainment and yes, ... for finding a job and building a successful career. From that small caravan of early cyberspace explorers in 1994, Internet usage grew to over 30 million people by 1997, a ten-fold increase in less than a thousand days! In addition, another 35.5 million Americans have access to the Internet at home or work and aren't yet users. As a consequence, there is every likelihood that the population of Internet users will double to over 65 million—almost 30% of all Americans—before the arrival of the new Millennium.

Where did this startling transformation come from and how will it affect our lives? What will the Internet do to the world of work and how will it change the way we find a job and manage our careers?

The answers to those questions are rooted in three startling changes that occurred in the United States in 1991. Ironically, these incidents received very little publicity or notice in the press. Yet, in many respects, they were watershed events, for they signaled this country's transition from an industrial era to a new social and economic age, a period I call the Electronic Era. It's not a very catchy name, but it is an accurate description of what is going on.

Change and Revolution

In 1991, for the very first time, the cost of the microelectronics in your car exceeded the cost of the metal with which it was made. On the average, you paid for $782 worth of electronic gadgetry and just $675 for the steel (*Fortune*, April 4, 1994). And that's just the beginning! From now on, when you purchase that quintessential expression of the American lifestyle—a car—you'll be spending more money on electronics in the engine and on the dashboard than on anything else.

There's been a similar revolution underway in virtually every other aspect of American living. American homes and recreation have been changed forever by the electronics in the television sets we watch, the microwave we use to cook our meals, the video games that captivate our kids (and some of us, as well), by our compact disc players, boom boxes, and the hand-held tape players we listen to while we jog. Electronics help us communicate by cellular telephones and pagers and through hearing aids and by TDD devices. Electronics have created a new era in our country, and that period is indisputably shaping the lives of all of us through the convenience and pleasure provided by its products.

It should not be surprising, therefore, that electronics have also begun to shape the world of work, as well. Indeed, in that same pivotal year of 1991, U.S. companies and corporations, for the very first time, spent more money on computers and telecommunications systems than they did on manufacturing, mining, construction and other equipment. And as remarkable as that milestone was, 1991 marked an even more significant event in cyberspace. That very same year, a protocol was accepted among the industrialized nations which transformed the Internet from a cranky network of interconnected research computers into a World Wide Web of instantaneous links, offering pictures and graphics and Web-sites and home pages. The intersection of those two events has redefined and reshaped American business ever since.

On the production line, robots now make more products to a higher standard of quality than we ever achieved in the Industrial Era. In retail companies, high speed management information systems are reducing the time and work required to identify customer preferences and to deliver the most popular products to store shelves. In service firms, the personal computer, the copier and the facsimile machine have reduced transaction times and improved flexibility, so that services can be customized to the specific needs of each client. And in companies large and small, competing in virtually every segment of the economy and operating in huge facilities, small retail outlets and home offices all over the United States and around the world, the Internet has opened new channels for sending and receiving information, conducting research, promoting products and services, communicating with customers and suppliers, and buying and selling both goods and services. As a result, electronics—in computers and computer networks—have helped make U.S. companies more competitive and increasingly successful in both our domestic economy and the global marketplace.

These changes, however, are not confined to the impersonal and distant arena of corporate strategy and economic competition. They have had an impact on each of us, as well. We shop in downtown malls where we leave our cars in parking lots managed by electronic ticketing machines and in on-line malls where we can see and order merchandise from the comfort of our homes. We obtain our spending money from automatic teller machines and do our banking, pay our mortgage, trade stocks and even order tickets from commercial Web-sites. We use electronic pagers and cell phones to keep us in touch with our office and the Internet to send and receive e-mail from our team members and suppliers, customers and prospects. Electronics make it all so easy and convenient that most of us have grown comfortable with their presence and dependent upon their benefits.

Indeed, the impact of the Electronic Era on our daily commerce is so pervasive as to be unremarkable. It's just there. The devices change from time-to-time, but mostly we've accepted that we live in an age when computer chips, miniaturized circuits and high speed processors will let us build things better, provide services more effectively and enjoy life more fully than ever before.

Unfortunately, however, it's not that simple. The Electronic Era has also begun to have a profound impact on our jobs and on the workplace and there, the changes are not so clearly beneficial.

The very same products of the Electronic Era that have made our homes and leisure pursuits so enjoyable and American companies so competitive are dramatically reshaping the world of work, as well. Processes and procedures and relationships and responsibilities are changing significantly. As a consequence, the workplace and the job market of the 1990's are unlike any that you and I have ever seen before.

The New Workplace

Part of this change is painful, as we know from the news each day. Computers and management information systems have eliminated tens of thousands of white collar middle management jobs. Scanners, inventory control systems, and robots have cut just as many blue collar positions. These changes are permanent. They are not the result of a recession or a temporary economic downturn. Instead, they are the signs of a dramatic restructuring in the way we work. The resulting lay-offs, reductions-in-force, downsizings and re-engineering programs have touched millions of Americans and left them uncertain about their security and opportunity in the future.

At the very same time, however, the electronics embedded in new technology are creating millions of new jobs. Contrary to popular notions, these positions are neither menial nor unpleasant, but instead, are high wage, high skill jobs offering great challenge and impressive rewards. The Hudson Institute, in its publication *Workforce 2020*, notes that 9.4 million net new jobs were created between 1989 and 1996. And another study found that 68% of all new jobs paid above-median wages. Or to put it another way, half of the new jobs actually pay better than 70% of all of the other jobs in the economy.

In fact, according to the U.S. Bureau of Labor Statistics, we are now in the middle of a huge wave of "good job" creation. The Bureau projects that, by 2005, the American economy will offer you and me and our kids about 144.7 million jobs, or some 17.7 million more jobs than existed in 1994. That's a gain of almost 14%, and the fastest segment of this growth will be in white collar positions. Professional jobs will increase by 29%, and jobs in the service sector will expand by 23%. In short—if you believe the projections—the Electronic Era is a "good job" generator.

These new jobs, however, create a new kind of job market. It is a job market characterized by paradox because it is simultaneously fraught with danger and brimming with opportunity. It is as different from the job market of the 1980's as carbon paper is from copiers.

This job market imposes its own unique set of rules. The techniques for conducting a successful job search campaign today are completely different from those that worked and worked well just five years ago. Indeed, if you try to find a new or better job in the new job market using the old rules of job hunting circa the 1980's, you will expose your career to considerable risk and deny yourself extraordinary employment opportunity. Conduct your job search using the new rules, however, and today's job market will create an almost unimaginable array of new possibilities to advance yourself in the world of work.

The New Job Market

I call this new job market "employment hyperspace." It is a jarring, fast-paced environment of job destruction and job creation, unlike any seen since the evolution of the United States from an agrarian to an industrial society. In the Industrial Era, for example, an organization's reputation was based on how big it was, and size was usually measured in the number of employees. In the Electronic Era, on the other hand, global competition and shareholder demands have changed the metric of success. Today, an organization is regarded not by its size, but by its efficiency, a characteristic most often denominated in terms of how much money it makes or how much value it provides. As a result, organizations have thrown themselves into crash diets that have shed millions of jobs. The sociology of today's corporation is increasingly oriented toward flatter organizational structures with fewer employees at higher skill levels. And since competitive pressures continue unabated, there is every likelihood that this "leaner, meaner" mindset will continue throughout the 1990's and beyond.

In addition, technological innovation is redesigning whole organizations and occupational fields as well as individual jobs. Hundreds of thousands of positions are being replaced with a much smaller number of self-directed jobs with higher skill requirements. For example, manufacturing technology is destroying a growing number of the positions that used to call for a person with a strong back and the basic reading, writing and arithmetic skills provided by a high school education. In their place, it is producing a dazzling array of new jobs that call for special skills in computer operation, electronic troubleshooting and higher order computational skills. Similarly, advanced information management systems are replacing white collar positions that were best suited for individuals who were adept at interpreting rules, implementing procedures and adhering to policy with jobs that call for individuals with special skills in problem solving, teamwork and innovation. For those men and women who have such skills or acquire them, the prospect is for secure employment at higher levels of pay than were ever achieved in the Industrial Era. For those who don't, on the other hand, the future is likely to be grim indeed.

As if this volatile mix weren't challenge enough, the modern workplace has also become wildly unpredictable. Today, virtually every working man and woman—people who have a job as well as those who are seeking one—must worry about being blindsided by the sale of their company, the closing of their plant, the introduction of a new machine that will replace them or a corporate strategy that will eliminate their job. These seemingly random events stimulate our anxiety, undercut our morale and discourage our trust in the organizations which employ us.

They do not leave us helpless, however. If you understand the forces that are shaping today's workplace and what they mean, you can recognize their impact in today's job market. If you see these forces not only for what they are but for what they can be; you can get out ahead of them and put them to work in your search for a new or better job. And if you harness those forces to your career, you can be in charge of the changes they are creating, rather than their victim.

So, how have these forces rippling through the workplace influenced the way you find a new or better job? What exactly are the characteristics of this new, Electronic Era job market?

Basically, there are three key features:

- Warp speed opportunities,

- High definition jobs, and

- Free agency.

Once you understand these unique differences, you'll have the foundation for successful job hunting and career management in the 1990's.

Warp Speed Opportunities

In the Industrial Era, finding a good job was a challenge best described as "here today, gone tomorrow." You had to move quickly to find, win and keep the job you wanted. In the Electronic Era, however, the nature of your job search has changed dramatically. Today, finding a good job is best described as "here today, gone in nanoseconds." Now, you have to move at warp speed if you want to win the job of your dreams.

The impact of electronics and other advances in technology have reduced the life cycle of a product to just 18 months. As a result, all of the jobs associated with each product—those in manufacturing, sales, marketing, distribution, even management—don't last much longer. What's that mean for you? Well, in the Industrial Era, you could probably count on changing jobs two, three maybe even four times during your career. In the Electronic Era, in contrast, everything happens faster. According to the U.S. Bureau of Labor Statistics, it's now far more likely that you'll experience seven-to-ten job changes and perhaps as many as fifteen-to-twenty during your career. Indeed, you may even change careers three-to-five times! Indeed, the only thing that's permanent about the new job market is change.

The symbol for career management in the Industrial Era was the gold watch. The idea was that you went to work for a single employer, spent virtually all of your career there and eventually retired from that organization. Your reward for all of those dedicated years of service was a gold watch and a good pension, if you were lucky.

In today's Electronic Era, on the other hand, the symbol for career management is not the gold watch, but the electronic remote control you use to change television channels. Today, tomorrow and into the next century, you will click rapidly through jobs, taking from each position the opportunity it presents to hone your skills and refine your capabilities in your chosen field of work and giving to each position and employer the benefit and value of that expanding competency. Although there will always be exceptions to the rule, it's far more likely that you will change jobs and employers regularly and therefore retire from your profession, craft or trade rather than from a career spent with just one organization.

High Definition Jobs

As technology roars into all corners of the workplace, the specific skills required for job performance become more exact and specific. The pace of technological development has become so rapid that 50% of your occupational skills now grow obsolete every three-to-five years. That means, of course, that you must view yourself as a work-in-progress. Your education and training are never done in the Electronic Era. Instead, you're always involved in acquiring new skills for the job you have today and for the new job you will inevitably have in the future.

These new skills are essential to high caliber job performance. Today, your co-worker on the job is, more often than not, a technologically advanced system or piece of equipment. To do your part and meet your responsibilities, you have to know how to interact with that technology and work with it on-the-job. As each piece of equipment and technology requires a specific set of skills, employers are becoming increasingly detailed about the array of capabilities and experiences that a person must have to be considered qualified for their open positions.

In fact, this specialization of competencies has changed the basic nature of recruiting. In the industrial era, when many jobs were similar and technology was much less intrusive in the design of jobs, the rule of thumb for successful recruiting was to "get the round peg in the round hole." Although not everyone could fit into every job (square pegs just didn't fit into round holes), the basic premise was that all round pegs were alike and so were all round jobs. In essence, people were interchangeable to a great degree.

In the Electronic Era, however, recruiting takes a fundamentally different approach. Now, many jobs are so different and unique, that recruiting for them is like opening a lock. Employers believe that only a very special person with a very specific set of qualifications can be the right person to open the lock. No less important, they are willing to wait until they find just that person—the single person with the precise set of skills they want—to fill their open position. Hence, the more specialized and more up-to-date your occupational credentials, the higher the probability that you will be competitive for the jobs being created in the new job market.

Free Agency

In the Industrial Era, you could count on your employer to manage your career for you. Particularly if you worked for a big company, you knew that the organization would (a) place you in a career path that defined your opportunity in the organization, (b) select and assign you to those jobs that would optimize your contribution to the organization, (c) ensure that you were trained for the jobs you held, and (d) move you along your career path to the appropriate level for your maximum contribution and achievement. All you had to do was be loyal and work hard. Your employer took care of everything else.

It was a very paternalistic system, and although there was precious little room for individuality and flexibility, many people found it to be a comfortable and reasonably secure arrangement. In the Electronic Era, however, companies have neither the resources nor the inclination to continue playing such a role. The competition is too tough and budgets are too tight for organizations to be able to manage the careers of their employees. Instead, in the Electronic Era, everyone is on their own.

As a result, from now on, you will have two jobs in the world of work: (1) to be a state-of-the-art performer in the high definition jobs you want in your chosen occupational field and (2) to manage your career so that you have the qualifications you need to compete for and win those warp speed jobs when you want them. That means:

- it's **your** job to select the positions that will provide you with the greatest challenge and opportunity;

- it's **your** job to get the skills and experience you need to compete for those positions;

- it's **your** job to find out where those positions are located; and

- it's **your** job to make sure that the employers which have those positions available know who you are and what qualifications you have to offer.

In essence, you are a free agent **and** the manager of your own career. You have unprecedented freedom and total responsibility.

A World of New Opportunities

The Electronic Era is producing monumental change in the way we live our lives and in the way we work. It is altering the nature of the jobs we hold and creating a new job market. This "employment hyperspace" can look and feel like chaos, but it's not. Instead, the new job market is an explosion of opportunity. As with any explosion, the jolt can be hurtful; if that energy is carefully managed, however, it can also be a force for opening new avenues of individual growth and career success.

That's the challenge you and I face in the new job market. The Electronic Era is destroying millions of Industrial Era jobs and simultaneously replacing them with millions of exciting, new positions. Hence, it holds both great danger and extraordinary rewards. Fail to see the danger or control its impact on your career, and you will seriously hurt your ability to find, win and keep the jobs you want in the 1990's. If you recognize the danger, on the other hand, and learn how to put its energy to work for your career, you will gain a huge competitive advantage in the job market.

Avoiding the danger and capturing the opportunity of the Electronic Era job market require a whole array of new skills for managing your career and conducting a job search successfully. How do you survive and prosper in such an environment? The chapter which follows will discuss these new skills.

11

The 5 Rules For Surviving & Prospering in the World of Work

There are five rules to success in the Electronic Era. At first, they are very likely to seem a bit strange and even feel uncomfortable to you. That's because they are different, not because they are wrong. These new rules were designed for today's and tomorrow's job market; they are unlike anything you may have learned about finding a job in the old Industrial Era. And that's entirely appropriate because, by-and-large, that old job market is gone forever.

New Rules and Big Benefits

The rules for surviving and prospering in the dynamic Electronic Era job market are:

Rule 1:	Keep Your Credentials in Constant Circulation
Rule 2:	Distribute Your Credentials as Broadly as Possible
Rule 3:	Practice Perpetual Documentation With Your Resume
Rule 4:	Exercise Total Control Over Your Job Search
Rule 5:	Lead With Your Strengths By Building Career Fitness

Each of these rules is described below. If you follow them, you'll gain two advantages. First, they will help you to plug into the employment hyperspace of the 1990's and the 21st century and second, they will give you a way to connect with the job opportunities that are being created at warp speed in your hometown, your state and region and in every corner of the United States and around the world. As a result, you will:

1. dramatically increase the number and quality of jobs available to you

2. ensure that you are seriously considered for those which are of interest to you.

The benefits of those two advantages are substantial. First, they will create a safety net of continuous employment opportunity for you. You'll be under constant consideration for great job openings just in case your current job disappears, for whatever reason. Indeed, as you will shortly see, this approach enables you to be more proactive, to anticipate threats to your current employment and do something about them, even while you are still at work on-the-job. In effect, your job search doesn't begin from a standing start, with all of the delays and frustrations that lack of preparation involves. Instead, your hunt for a new or better opportunity is already underway, in high gear, so that you are already well on your way to finding what you want while others are still getting organized and figuring out what to do. Like a "career insurance" policy, it's always there and it's always ready, if and when you need it.

Second, being engaged in today's employment hyperspace is a smart way to advance your career. Unfortunately, the movement to flatter organizations among U.S. companies has significantly diminished the opportunity for upward mobility. Hence, in many cases today, the only way to get ahead is to seek a new position in a different organization. If there is still room for you to grow in your current employer's organization, that's great. Take advantage of it. But if there is no position in which you can improve yourself and advance your level of expertise and experience with your current employer, then it is your responsibility as your own career manager to look elsewhere. And to do that, you need to plug into the Electronic Era job market and connect with its employment opportunities.

RULE 1: Keep Your Resume in Constant Circulation

The first requirement of the Electronic Era job market is to keep your resume in constant circulation. When you're employed and when you're not. You must always have your resume out there among prospective employers so that they know who you are and what qualifications you can offer to them on-the-job.

In the Industrial Era, it was considered disloyal to put your resume out into the job market while you were employed. In the new job market, however, the definition of loyalty has expanded. Now, you must be loyal to your employer **and** you must be loyal to yourself. The loyalty that you owe to your employer is to deliver the best performance you can in your job, not to remain employed in that job or with that organization forever.

The loyalty that you owe to yourself and your family is to protect your ability to work and earn a living. Indeed, in the Electronic Era job market, loyalty to yourself is a matter of survival. You need to insulate yourself from job changes initiated by your employer and you need to find new career opportunities that will protect and enhance your financial security and employability. Moreover, most career counselors have long agreed that the best time to find a new job is not when you are out of work, but rather, while you are still employed. And the best way to do that is to keep your work credentials in circulation all of the time.

So, in the Electronic Era job market, you have to find a way to keep your resume in circulation regardless of your circumstances, obligations, activities and constraints. You must have your resume out there where employers can see it even though you are still at work in your current position. And you must get beyond the limitations of your own time and energy and keep your resume on-the-job while you are on vacation, running errands, even while you're asleep. In other words, constant circulation means putting your resume to work 24 hours a day, 7 days a week, 365 days a year. It is a full time process that must never stop.

RULE 2: Distribute Your Credentials as Broadly as Possible

The best way to keep your resume in circulation is to broadcast it as widely as possible. Even if you think that you will never move outside your current community or take a job in an industry other than the one in which you now work, it's critical that you **not** limit the range of your resume's distribution. Why? Because you just can't predict what might happen. In the Electronic Era job market, exciting new opportunities can appear anywhere and at any time. The only way to ensure that you will even know about them is to keep your resume circulating as widely as possible. You can always turn a position down if you decide it's not right for you, but you'll never have that opportunity (or, more importantly, the chance to accept that job), if the employer simply hasn't heard of you. So, the best rule of thumb for circulating your resume in the 1990's is to accept absolutely no impediments to or impose any limits on where it goes. The further afield the better.

Of course, that means you should continue to do all of the things that you have traditionally done to get your resume into circulation:

- answer recruitment ads in newspapers and other publications,

- use the telephone to prospect for job openings with employers,

- contact headhunters and other recruiters who specialize in your field, and

- network among your friends and colleagues.

In the Electronic Era job market, however, doing all of that is important, but it's not enough. Too many other job seekers are in the market doing the same things. Hence, you have to do something else to increase the range of your resume and to put it into niches of the job market with which you are not personally familiar. Your goal is to connect with what's called "the hidden job market."

This invisible job market encompasses the vast number of employment positions which are never advertised and hence remain unknown to most people. Ironically, these are some the best available positions, great jobs that are filled without a lot of public fanfare or knowledge. One of the keys to success in the Electronic Era job market, therefore, is to ensure that your credentials get considered for as many of these hidden jobs as possible. And circulating your resume broadly is one of the best ways to make that happen.

RULE 3: Practice Perpetual Documentation With Your Resume

In the old job market of the Industrial Era, most people didn't expect to change jobs with any degree of frequency, so they seldom prepared themselves in advance for a job search. That usually meant that you didn't "do your resume" until you were actually out of work and in the job market. At that point, however, developing a resume became a monumental effort under great pressure. Job opportunities were being lost while you slogged your way through (1) learning or re-learning the skills required for writing a good resume, (2) making decisions about your job search objective, (3) identifying the appropriate skills and experience you should document on your resume in support of that objective, and (4) creating a final document that would work effectively for you in the job market. The whole process slowed down the pace of your job search and delayed your return to the financial security and other benefits of employment.

An out-of-date resume was harmful enough in the Industrial Era job market, but in the Electronic Era job market, it can be fatal. Since success in today's job market requires that you keep your resume in constant circulation, you must always have such a document at the ready, and it must always be complete and up-to-date. Indeed, from now on, your resume must be a living document. It must be current and accurate. And, it must record changes in your skills, abilities, and experience at the moment they occur.

There's no other way to compete for the jobs you want in the Electronic Era job market. Jobs come and go too fast. An out-of-date resume simply will not represent you well in the fierce competition for the great jobs in today's employment hyperspace. In fact, it signals a level of personal carelessness and irresponsibility from which any employer will shy away. So, to make sure you aren't overlooked or under-evaluated for the employment opportunities of the 1990's, you must always have a comprehensive, up-to-the-minute resume in circulation.

RULE 4: Exercise Total Control Over Your Job Search

In the Industrial Era job market, job seekers were warned to exercise continuous control over the distribution of their resume. You were exhorted to know, at all times, where your resume was being sent and for what opportunity. Such control was the only way that you could ensure the confidentiality of your job search, and that confidentiality was the only way you could protect yourself from an embarrassing and potentially dangerous situation with your current employer.

The same is true of the Electronic Era job market. Confidentiality preserves your freedom in the job market. Indeed, it may be even more important today, given your need to keep your resume in circulation all of the time and as broadly as possible. That strategy is the only way you can stay abreast of the warp speed opportunities being created in the employment hyperspace of the Electronic Era. Its success, however, depends, in large measure, on your ability to broadcast your resume anywhere and everywhere without having to worry about its landing on your boss's desk.

Further, you want to be sure that you are considered only for the jobs that are of interest to you. Total control over the circulation of your resume protects you from the potentially negative consequences of being considered for the wrong job. Nothing upsets a prospective employer more than to spend the time and energy required to evaluate a candidate seriously for an open job, only to discover later that he/she has no interest in it. When that situation occurs, it makes the candidate look unprofessional and even inconsiderate—not the kind of reputation that will stand you in good stead in subsequent job searches.

Consequently, any loss of control in the job market can hurt you badly. You cannot take too many precautions to ensure that your job search is private and that you determine where and when you will be considered for an open position. On the other hand, exercising proactive control can pay handsome dividends in the number and quality of opportunities for which you are considered in the Electronic Era job market.

RULE 5: Lead With Your Strengths By Building Career Fitness

The first four rules above are key principles that will help you to connect with the employment opportunities being created every day in the Electronic Era job market. They will not, however, ensure that you capture those opportunities; they will not, by themselves, enable you to win the jobs you want.

You can put your resume in circulation all of the time, you can broadcast it widely in the job market, you can keep your resume up-to-date and remain in total control of your job search and still come away empty handed. Why?

Because your appeal to prospective employees is based on the **strength** of your occupational skills, not your talent for distributing your resume. If your resume describes a brain dead worker, you can circulate it as broadly as you like, but it won't do you a lot of good. You won't be of any interest to any of the employers with open positions to fill.

To help you to identify and build your occupational strengths, I developed a concept called "Career Fitness." As with physical fitness, improving your career fitness is something that only you can do and that you must work on all of the time. It's your responsibility to manage your career, and it's a job that's every bit as important as the one you do for your employer. It's the best way to build job security for yourself and to enhance the paycheck and the satisfaction that you bring home from work each day.

I have collected the exercises or techniques for building Career Fitness into a "Career Fitness Workout." Collectively, they are designed to help you achieve a single, critical goal: to **Be Your Personal Best** in the field of work you most enjoy. To attain that level of excellence, you must keep your skills at the state-of-the-art in your occupation and acquire new capabilities—valued added skills in oral and written communications and foreign languages; in financial management and other aspects of running a business; in computer literacy, word processing and spreadsheet analysis; and in leadership, particularly among a diverse workforce organized and operating in teams—that will improve the impact of your work. When you have these kinds of occupational strengths and you document them in your resume and circulate it broadly and constantly in the job market, you'll have an enormous advantage in finding, winning and keeping the jobs you want in the 1990's.

For a complete guide to building Career Fitness in the Electronic Era, please see my book, *Career Fitness: How to Find, Win & Keep the Job You Want in the 1990's* (Cadell & Davies, 1994). You can purchase the book from me (I'll even sign it) at its retail price of $19.95, plus $4.95 shipping, a total of $24.90. Just send your name, address and check or money order payable to Peter D. Weddle, 292 Sound Beach Avenue, Unit 1, Old Greenwich, CT 06870.

The next sections of the book will tell you how you can put these new rules of the Electronic Era job market to work for you. Chapter 12 will introduce you to "electronic networking," a technique you can use to plug into the employment hyperspace of the Electronic Era. Chapter 13 will show you how to use your electronic resume for electronic networking with computerized Human Resource Departments, employment agencies and search firms. Chapter 14 will show you how to use your Internet resume for electronic networking with Web-sites operated by employers and by commercial employment companies, professional associations and other not-for-profit organizations. Chapter 15 will show you how to pick the best employment Web-sites on the Internet so you can take the Net to your next job, and Chapter 16 will introduce you to "Weddle's Picks," twenty of the best employment Web-sites currently operating on the Internet and the World Wide Web.

12

Electronic Networking

The conventional wisdom in the Industrial Era job market was simple: the best way to find a good job was through networking. That convention recognized the fact that many open positions and certainly most of the best opportunities were not advertised in the newspapers. They were, instead, a part of the "hidden job market."

To uncover the employment opportunities in the "hidden job market," you had to talk to people who knew about them or who knew the hiring managers in the organizations where they were located. Those contacts, in turn, enabled you to get your credentials into the competition. They would help you find the open jobs available in the hidden job market. Hence, the more people you contacted—the more networking you did—the better the odds that you would connect with that one person who knew about the right position for you.

Discover a New World of Networking

In the Industrial Era, the way you networked was with your Rolodex. If you had a job and weren't, at that particular moment, looking for something new or better (remember, showing such initiative was considered bad form), you kept your contacts "warm" by staying in touch with them as frequently as

153

you could. You saw them at the annual meeting of your professional or trade association; you did lunch together; you chatted on the phone or you traded a letter every now and then. In short, you did what you could to build a face-to-face relationship with a circle of friends and colleagues on which you could count.

Why? Because when you were unemployed or looking for a new or better job, the first thing you did, in the Industrial Era at least, was "run your traps." You started looking for employment opportunities in the hidden job market by talking to as many people as possible, starting with friends and colleagues. It was analogous to setting out a long line of traps in hopes that you would catch a great job that was hidden in the market. You would telephone or meet with the people whom you knew who would then refer you to a second tier of people whom you would, in turn, contact who would then refer you to a third tier of possibilities and so on. Eventually, if all went according to convention, you would find a great job that was just right for you. The key to successful networking in the Industrial Era, therefore, was that Rolodex; the more people whom you knew, the better the odds of finding your special job.

In the Electronic Era, however, networking is different. Given the dynamics of today's job market, the best way to network now is not to increase the number of people whom you know, but rather to expand the number of people who know you. The greater the number of people who are aware of your credentials and qualifications, the higher the probability that you will be selected for an employment opportunity. The key to successful networking in the Electronic Era job market, therefore, is your resume. You must find a way to increase the reach and visibility of your credentials.

And that's the rub. Conventional networking is a face-to-face exercise, limited to the number of people with whom you can stay in touch. It's very labor intensive and depends entirely on you. The more time and effort you spend, the greater the number of contacts you have. Unfortunately, you and I and everyone else only have so much time to offer. There are other things going on in our lives. We need to eat from time-to-time. We need to sleep, go to work, spend time with our families and friends. Yet, when we're doing those things, we diminish the time we have available to work at our networking.

Yet, work is precisely what networking is all about! Just as the word, itself, states, connecting with the hidden job market is net**work**, not net-play or net-relax. Indeed, in the Electronic Era, your networking should be an integral and regular part of every workday. It is, in essence, now a fundamental component of your occupation and your career.

Success in the Electronic Era job market is dependent upon your finding a way to overcome these limitations imposed on your own time so that you can increase the number of people who know about you. Fortunately, the same electronics that have imposed so many changes on our lifestyles and our workplace have also created a solution to this dilemma. This solution captures the power and speed of advanced technology and harnesses it to the task of broadcasting your credentials throughout the hidden job market. It's the difference between running your own little circle of traps by foot and beaming at warp speed through an even bigger circuit by using electronic technology. Hence, I call this technique "electronic networking."

Now, don't give up on networking by foot. In fact, electronic networking is actually a method to augment the networking you can and should do on your own. It is not a substitute for conventional networking or for responding to classified ads or any of the traditional strategies for finding a job. Instead, it is a new and powerful technique that you can **add to** these tried-and-true techniques to improve the effectiveness and success of your job search.

So, how does electronic networking work? Basically, it puts your resume into circulation through a computer. The computer then matches your work credentials with the requirements specified for open jobs and connects you with the appropriate employer. It's still up to you to land the job, but the computer has opened the door for you and "made the introduction," usually to an employer whom you do **not** know, but who, thanks to the computer, now knows you. Hence, electronic networking provides the same benefit as conventional networking—it puts you in touch with more of the employment opportunities in the hidden job market—but it does so in the blink of an eye and to places far beyond where you can reach on foot.

Learn to "See"

Electronic networking, however, has an additional advantage. It enables you to **SEE**. Electronic networking gives you visibility in the job market and access to employment opportunities in a way that is **S**afe, **E**fficient and **E**ffective.

Safe: Electronic networking is safe because you can control where and when the computer makes a match for you. The computer does all of the work, but you're still in charge.

Effective: Electronic networking is effective because it expands the range of positions you can contact beyond those available to you in the classified ads and through your own conventional networking. In addition, it can connect you with the vast array of unadvertised employment opportunities in the "hidden job market" and

Efficient: Electronic networking is efficient because that computer never has to sleep, eat or take a rest. Hence, it enables you to connect with employment opportunities anywhere in the world—from your hometown to Paris, London, Sydney or Tokyo, it's up to you—24 hours a day, 7 days a week, 365 days a year. Electronic networking connects you with the hidden job market while you're on another job interview, while you're at work in your current job, even while you're on vacation or taking a nap on the sofa.

Acquire a Special Edge

Electronic networking gives you a special edge by putting the power of advanced technology to work for you. It enables you to work smart as well as work hard to build a successful and rewarding career. In essence, it creates a new kind of distribution system for your resume that will plug you into the Electronic Era job market.

Electronic networking happens two ways:

1. **When using your electronic resume to input your qualifications into:**

   ■ the resume management systems used by employers,

   ■ the computerized databases used by employment agencies and search firms, and

- the off-line (non-Internet) computers feeding the on-line resume databases operated by employment Web-sites.

2. **When using your Internet resume to input your qualifications into:**

- the on-line application forms feeding the on-line resume databases operated by employment Web-sites, and

- an e-mail response to employers' job listings on their own Web-sites or posted in an employment Web-site's jobs database.

The next two chapters will describe these two forms of electronic networking in detail.

13

How to Use Your Electronic Resume to Do Electronic Networking

Today, electronic networking is possible, in part, because of the widespread growth of computers among employers and recruiters. On the one hand, virtually every company in the Fortune 1000 and an increasing number of small and mid-sized organizations now use computerized resume management systems to store, search and retrieve the resumes of prospective employment candidates. On the other hand, a significant and growing number of employment agencies and search firms now maintain computerized candidate databases to store individual resumes and profiles and even the notes that were made about candidates in previous interviews and interactions. In essence, the world of recruiting is being transformed into an electronic environment, and you must be able to connect with and participate in this environment or risk being overlooked and forgotten in the job market.

Electronic Technology

Your electronic resume is your ticket into this new electronic world of recruiting. But to use it effectively, you need to have at least some knowledge of how the technology in this environment actually works.

Basically, a resume management system and a computerized database of candidate profiles use the same technology. They both combine computer hardware and software into an integrated system which enables a recruiter to (a) store resumes or other employment-related information in an automated database; (b) search among all of the resumes/employment information in the database and identify those files that meet specific criteria; (c) review the information contained in the files and, if desired, print it out in paper form; and then (d) return the files to the database for future use. As noted above, in some cases, the technology will also permit the recruiter to add comments, notes from telephone calls and interviews and other supplementary information obtained through interaction with the candidates.

Resume management systems and computerized databases have impressive capabilities, but they are also very expensive. Off-the-shelf systems can cost from $10,000 to over $100,000, while customized systems can run $250,000 or more. So, why do organizations buy them? What makes acquring such technology so appealing to large and small employers, alike?

The answer, in a word, is paper. Paper costs money, consumes resources and causes problems. And organizations today are being flooded with paper resumes. These documents require huge areas of space to store. They are time consuming to search—which can only be done manually—and the search process, itself, is prone to error. In addition, paper degrades with age, making it difficult to use for any extended period of time; and paper resumes cannot be easily updated or revised by candidates to reflect their changing qualifications. Hence, when employers, employment agencies and search firms decide to adopt technology in the recruiting process, they are usually making a commitment to eliminate or, at least, dramatically reduce their use of paper resumes.

Moving to an electronic environment gives these organizations a number of immediate and important advantages. First, it is easy and efficient to store resumes in a computer. A single desktop PC can have the memory to hold literally tens of thousands of resumes in its database. Second, these databases are easy to search, and the search process is both fast and highly accurate. The computer searches the database by reading every word in every resume it contains and does the job in a matter of seconds. And third, the information that is stored in a database does not degrade and is easily updated so that candidate files are often more comprehensive and current.

These advantages, in turn, can translate into significant productivity gains and performance improvements for an organization. They can reduce the time and cost to recruit and raise the quality of the candidates considered for the organization's job openings. Those benefits are key assets in today's fast-paced and highly competitive staffing environment. They are the return that justifies the substantial investment required to implement a resume management system or a computerized candidate database.

Using Your Electronic Resume to Do Electronic Networking

Electronic networking involves two linked steps: getting in the door and getting recognized for what you can do. The format of your electronic resume is specifically designed to help you take the first step, while its content will enable you to take the second.

Getting in the Door

Organizations which decide to install a resume management system or a computerized database have three options. They can purchase an "off the shelf" product, such as Resumix, Restrac, SmartSearch2 and others. They can develop their own customized version, using commercially available hardware and software. Or they can send their resumes out to a "processing house" which will, for a fee, input them into a database which the organization can then access, either on-line or on its own computer.

Whatever the approach, however, virtually all resume management systems and computerized databases use a device called a scanner to input resumes. As discussed earlier, scanners apply a technology called "optical character recognition" or OCR which converts the image of your resume into digitized information which the computer can accept and understand. Although OCR software has vastly improved in the last five years, it still has great difficulty deciphering italics, underlining, shading, fancy typefaces and graphics—in short, all of the devices typically used to catch the human eye on a conventional paper resume. When a scanner "sees" such images it either creates a garbled, often unintelligible version of the resume or it simply rejects it. In either case, your effort to present your credentials to that organization has been effectively derailed.

When you use an electronic resume, however, the scanner likes what it sees. The format of your electronic resume is specifically designed to complement the capabilities of scanners, so its processing is fast and effective. The scanner takes a clear and accurate "picture" of your resume which is then translated into a standard text format that eliminates all of the spacing and "packs" the resume for storage. Then, your resume is moved into the database of the computer where it stored for subsequent searching and, hopefully, matches with the specifications for one or more job openings.

The scanner's successful processing of your electronic resume effectively gets your credentials in the employer's door. And thanks to the unique format of your electronic resume, those credentials are perfectly arrayed to highlight what you can do and how well you can do it:

- your most important credentials are up front at the beginning of your file in your Key Word Summary;

- your major sections and key information (i.e., the names of employers) are set off with capital letters; and

- your accomplishments are emphasized with bullets that the computer will recognize and accept.

Now, it's up to the content of your electronic resume to ensure that you are recognized for what you can do.

Getting Recognized For What You Can Do

Traditionally, resume books have strongly encouraged the use of action verbs in the content of conventional paper resumes. They advocate a very heavy dose of such words as "directed," "managed," "built," and "achieved" because these terms convey a sense of accomplishment when read by people, and paper resumes are designed to be reviewed by a human recruiter. Further, resume experts often caution against the use of technical terms and jargon (e.g., programming languages, finance and accounting or manufacturing terminology) in paper resumes because these words are often expressed as lists which are boring for people to read.

In an electronic resume, however, it is nouns and phrases and technical terms and jargon which give the document its power. As discussed earlier, organizations search their resume and candidate databases by entering a series of key words into the computer and telling it to look for matches to those words in its files. For example, the computer can be directed to look for every resume which contains the following nouns: "engineer," "civil," "California," and the computer will read every word in every resume to find those which do. Unfortunately, however, the computer is only as smart as the specificity of its instructions, so with this particular set of key words, it will also identify the resumes of those individuals who work in "civil affairs" and "civil law" and those who live on any "California Street" or "California Road" in the database. As a consequence, employers also use a set of connecting words called Boolean operators—terms such as "and," "or," and "but not"—which help to increase the specificity of their instructions. In this case, for example, the computer could be directed to look for the phrase "engineer and civil but not law or affairs" which would effectively require it to find civil engineers.

The content of your electronic resume is rich in such key nouns and phrases, and they optimize your chances of being identified in a database search. In addition, it also compensates for the great variability in the way different people express the same idea. For example, some recruiters will use the term "personnel administration" to describe the function of a job opening, while another will use the term "human resource management" to describe an identical position. Because your electronic resume expresses all of your ASSETS, it will include both the appropriate terms **and** the synonyms of those terms that describe your qualifications. As a result, your electronic resume has the right stuff to help you get recognized for what you can do.

When you can get in the door at those employers with open positions and be recognized for what you can do in those positions, you are effectively engaged in electronic networking. You can tap into the incredible employment opportunities being created in the employment hyperspace of the Electronic Era and you can SEE.

Safe: Your job search is safe because your confidentiality is protected. Your electronic resume is archived on the computer in an employer's Human Resource

Department or in the database at an employment agency or search firm. It is under control and out of public circulation so you don't have to worry about its landing on the wrong person's desk.

Effective: Your job search is effective because you will be considered for every single one of an organization's employment openings. The computer does not forget who is in its database nor does it selectively avoid one resume or another. Every word in every resume gets read by the computer for every job opening.

Efficient: Your job search will be efficient because you will be considered for the organization's job openings at all times, regardless of what you are doing. Your electronic resume is available to be searched in the organization's database and identified for a position vacancy 24 hours a day, 7 days a week, 365 days a year.

The next chapter will show you how to capture even more of the benefits of electronic networking by extending it into cyberspace. You will learn how to make your work record available to employers in your home town and all over the globe by sending your Internet resume to employment-related Web-sites.

It is important to note here, however, that some employment Web-sites, particularly those which serve a relatively specific segment of the workforce (e.g., specialty sites for specific occupations and sites maintained by professional associations and other affinity groups) build their on-line resume databases with off-line scanners and OCR technology. In essence, they accept paper resumes sent to them through the mail and convert these documents into data which is then transferred into an electronic recruiting environment on the Internet and the World Wide Web. Therefore, your electronic resume can also be used to input your credentials into these employment Web-sites, as well as the resume management systems and computerized databases discussed above.

14

How to Use Your Internet Resume to Do Electronic Networking

Internet employment sites represent the most exciting development in job search and career management in the last fifty years. These sites use the extraordinary capability of the Information Superhighway to put your employment credentials in front of hundreds of thousands of organizations with position vacancies located in your home town, your state or region and all over the globe. They connect you with the employment opportunities that are advertised in virtually every major newspaper in America and with those job openings which are a part of the "hidden job market." They enable you to look for a job whenever you want and wherever you want and even to be considered for employment opportunities while you're away from your computer and doing something else.

As always, responding to classified ads, telephone prospecting for open positions and other traditional job search activities will also put your credentials into circulation. You should continue to do all of these things, using your electronic resume, wherever appropriate. To them, however, you can now add the power and reach of the Internet and the World Wide Web. You can extend your job search into cyberspace.

There are two ways to tap into the on-line job market: the Web-sites maintained by employers and the Web-sites operated by commercial employment companies, not-for-profit organizations, educational institutions and other affinity groups.

Employers' Web-Sites

According to some estimates, there are now thousands of organizations which have established and maintain a site on the Internet and/or the World Wide Web. How do you determine who they are and locate their "address" or Universal Resource Locator (URL) on-line?

Basically, there are two ways to find out if and/or where an employer maintains a Web-site:

1. You can use what is called a "search engine" which is, in essence, an automated index of all or most of the sites on-line. There are a number of these indices, including AltaVista, InfoSeek, Lycos and Yahoo!. If you are new to the Internet and don't know which search engine to use, there is a good list of search engines available on-line at http://home.netscape.com/home/internet-search.html.

While each of these engines has its own particular features and strengths, they all essentially do the same thing. Search engines enable you to prospect through their listings of Internet sites by simply entering the name of the organization for which you are looking. There is one small problem, however. Since the search engine is designed to be as complete in its search as possible, it will list the address of every newspaper article, press release, and other reference to the organization as well as the address of its Web-site, if it has one. That means you may have to look through a lot of entries to find what you want.

2. You can use the Internet version of the phone book. There are a number of sites which provide a listing of employer contact information, including their Internet address, if they have one. Since organizations come and go and addresses change from time-to-time, no single one of these directories covers every employer which has an on-line site. Therefore, your best bet is to visit several and search their listings for information about the organization of interest to you.

Some of the best Internet directories include:

Address	**Description**
http://www.bigbook.com/	A directory of 16 million businesses
http://s13.bigyellow.com/	The NYNEX Yellow Pages
http://www.onvillage.com/	A national directory of 15 million businesses
http://www.superpages.gte.net/	A directory of 11 million listings drawn from over 5,000 Yellow Pages directories across the country
http://www.thomasregister.com/	The Thomas Register of American Manufacturers
http://yp.uswest.com	The US WEST Yellow Pages
http://www.whowhere.com/	An on-line Yellow Pages of 11 million companies
http://www.yp.ameritech.net/	The Ameritech Yellow Pages
http://yahoo.com/yahoo/yp.html	The Yahoo! Yellow Pages

As you will quickly learn, there is considerable variability in the purpose and sophistication of employer's Web-sites. Some of the sites contain little more than "brochureware" or promotional information about the products and services produced and/or sold by the organization. Other sites offer in-depth information about the history, culture, mission and performance of the organization as well as a virtual tour of its facilities and an audio message from its Chief Executive Officer.

In addition, a growing number of sites are now listing the position vacancies in the organization for both its operating units in the United States and those around the world. Typically, these listings present much more information than is available in a classified ad. Many will actually contain the full position description for the vacancy. They will also almost always:

- indicate if the position is full time, part time, contract or contingent,
- specify its salary level,
- provide contact information and, in a growing number of instances,
- permit you to submit your resume on-line.

Your Internet resume enables you to take advantage of this opportunity. In some cases, you will be asked to paste your resume into an e-mail message and send it to a designated recipient or address in the company. In other cases, you will be asked to paste it into an on-line application form which will often also ask for additional information not found on a resume (e.g., the date you are available to start work or your willingness to re-locate and/or to travel). Once completed, you simply click on the "submit" button and your credentials are hyperlinked directly to the organization's computer, where they can be downloaded and reviewed.

Although there is considerable variability in the way different employer's respond to such submissions, many have devised an automatic confirmation message which they will send to you by e-mail, once your Internet resume has arrived. If you don't receive such a message or some other acknowledgment from the employer in 3-5 days, I suggest that you send a simple request for confirmation. Since Internet communications are still occasionally lost in cyberspace, this message is a non-intrusive way to protect yourself from a pothole on the Information Superhighway.

To be effective, however, this request should be short and straight forward, such as:

Dear Sir/Madam:

On [date], I sent my resume to you via ["e-mail" or "your on-line enrollment form"] for ["job number ___" or "the position of _____"]. Would you please confirm by return e-mail that you have received my resume?

Sincerely,
Your Full Name
Your e-mail address
Your telephone number

You should also recognize that, although you submitted your credentials to the employer at warp speed over the Internet, the employer's process of candidate review and selection is still likely to be laborious and time consuming. Therefore, don't set yourself up for disappointment by expecting to hear something definitive from the employer twenty-four hours later. In most cases, that simply won't happen. And if it doesn't, don't bombard the organization with e-mail inquiries about the status of its search. Making yourself a pest is one of the quickest ways to find yourself eliminated from the competition.

Employment Web-Sites

There are now over 11,000 employment Web-sites operating on the Internet and more are being launched every day. They offer job seekers and others a wide array of assistance and support for job search and career management. Some sites post classified and display ads, others operate a job bank or a resume database, and still others provide all three. There are sites which offer on-line resume writing assistance, career counseling, and salary information and sites which have "hot links" or electronic connections to other sites which, themselves, provide useful resources for finding a job or building a successful career.

Many of the employment Web-sites cater to virtually anyone and everyone in the workforce, but some are very specialized or designed to assist the members of a particular group. For example, if you are a graduate of Dartmouth or Yale (or any of 13 other institutions of higher education) or the New York Institute of Technology Culinary Arts Program, the United States Military Academy or Purdue University, there's a special site for you; and if you're a member of the American Astronomical Association, the International Home Workers Association or the Society of Photo-Optical Instrumentation Engineers, there are special sites for you, as well.

There are also employment Web-sites which focus on certain occupational fields, selected industries and segments of the workforce and individuals at designated salary levels. For example, you can find employment sites for first-time job seekers, telecommuters and those making $75,000 a year or more; you can also find sites for Hispanic job seekers, African-American engineers, and those who speak English and at least one Asian language (Japanese, Chinese or Korean). There are sites for pilots, funeral directors, actors and journalists, doctors, ministers, women in high technology and those with MBA degrees; and there are sites which offer jobs in Ireland, Australia, Canada and New Jersey, Milwaukee, Syracuse, Philadelphia and Denver.

Despite this variability in the range of products and services these sites offer, almost all provide at least one and many provide all three of the following general categories of assistance:

- Resume circulation.
- Information and services for job search and/or career management.

■ Access to job openings.

On-line employment sites are a particularly effective way to circulate your work record, and your Internet resume enables you to take advantage of this capability. Currently, employment Web-sites offer everything from passive resume circulation, where your Internet resume is simply archived in a publicly accessible database, to more proactive capabilities which send your resume directly to an employer when it matches with the specified requirements for a job opening. For those who are currently employed and concerned about privacy, some employment Web-sites will permit you to "block" your resume from being sent to designated organizations (such as your current employer). And other sites offer a capability called "push technology" which will send you a notice, either in a private mailbox on their site or to your e-mail address, when your Internet resume has matched with a job opening. This notification enables you to decide—before an employer can obtain your name, contact information or resume—whether you are interested in the opportunity or the organization offering it.

There are a wide spectrum of employment Web-sites offering databases where you can post your Internet resume. For example, if you're looking for a full time position, you can use your Internet resume to post your work record at such sites as:

Site Name	Address/URL
America's Talent Bank	*http://www.atb.org*
CareerCity	*http:www.careercity.com*
CareerWeb	*http:www.cweb.com*
Westech's Virtual Job Fair	*http://vjf.com*
4Work	*http://4work.com*

On the other hand, if you're looking for a telecommuting job, you can post your resume at Telecommuting Jobs, *http://www.tjobs.com/index. html*, or if you're interested in contract employment, you can send your resume to the Contract Employment Connection, *http://www.ntes.com*, and it will send it to every technical service firm in the United States.

Within the category of information and services for job search and/or career management, today's sites offer some or all of the following kinds of assistance: career and occupational information, job market information, job search tips, resume writing assistance, salary guides, employer profiles, job search counseling, career counseling, hot links to other employment sites, and hot links to employer sites. The quality of this assistance varies widely and can range from magazine article reprints to interactive support from a certified expert, from detailed checklists and guides to superficial summaries, from resources developed by seasoned professionals to those offered by individuals and organizations with absolutely no expertise or track record in employment.

For example, you can get free advice on how to write a cover letter from the author of a book on the same subject by visiting CareerLab at *http://www.careerlab.com*. You can find a directory of executive recruiters at the Career Magazine site, *http://www.careermag.com*; chat with others who are also looking for a job on-line at Career Mart, *http://www.careermart.com*; post questions about benefits on a cyber bulletin board at BenefitsLink, *http://benefitslink.com/*; get free information about employers at Hoovers, *http://www.hoovers.com*; read the career advice of expert Joyce Lain Kennedy at The Monster Board, *http://www.monster.com*; and play "Stump the Mentor" at *Hard@Work, http://hardatwork.com*.

If, on the other hand, you're most interested in gaining access to job openings, there is a vast number of sites which can help you do that, as well. To take advantage of them, however, you have to be very clear and specific in your own mind about the nature of the job for which you are looking. Although many sites purport to offer a wide range of positions, most have databases which are strongest in one, two or, at most, three segments of the job market. Moreover, the quality of these opportunities varies a great deal. Some offer vacancies that are very current and therefore likely to be still open, while others are so out of date that they have already been filled. Some are "lifted" from other on-line and print sources, and some are provided exclusively to the site by an employer or recruiter and cannot be found elsewhere.

The most extensive database of open jobs is operated by the U.S. Department of Labor at a site called America's Job Bank, *http://www.ajb.dni.us*. It archives over 750,000 positions—including skilled technical jobs and even management level positions paying substantial salaries—gathered from state employment agencies. Other sites with large job databases include CareerPath at *http://www.careerpath.com*—which posts the Sunday classified ads from over fifty of the country's largest newspapers, ranging from the *Atlanta Journal-Constitution*, *Boston Globe*, *The Chicago Tribune*, and *The Denver Post*, to the *Los Angeles Times*, *Miami Herald* and *The New York Times*—as well as the following:

Site Name	Address/URL
Best Jobs U.S.A.	*http://www.bestjobsusa.com*
E-span	*http://www.espan.com*
Online Career Center	*http://www.occ.com*
PassportAccess	*http://www.passportaccess.com*

Once you've determined the kind(s) of assistance you want from an employment Web-site and its parameters, you need to make two additional decisions in order to select those sites which have the best capabilities for you:

- First, are you willing to pay for the resources provided by the site or do you want to use only those sites which offer resources at no cost to the individual?

- Second, are you willing to register with a site, which will require that you provide the site operator with some level information about yourself (other than that which is normally provided in a resume), in order to use its resources?

Those decisions and your specifications for how you want to use the site (i.e., to store your Internet resume, to acquire job search and career management information and services, and/or to look for job openings of interest to you) are your **baseline** for selecting an employment Web-site. The next step in taking the Net to a new or better job is to evaluate the range and quality of resources provided by various sites in order to determine which best meets your baseline requirements. Chapter 15 presents a comprehensive questionnaire which you can use to assess the capabilities of alternative employment Web-sites.

15

How to Evaluate an Employment Web-Site

Using on-line employment resources doesn't require a lot of advanced computer knowledge, but it does demand a certain level of shopping sophistication. There are many fine sites on the Internet and the World Wide Web that offer a wide array of information, products and services that can extend and enrich your job search campaign and your career. The challenge for you is to find which site with what resources best meets your need.

Virtually every employment Web-site in operation today touts itself as #1 in its particular niche or area of expertise. As good as many of these sites truly are, they all can't be the best. Indeed, while some sites provide world class support to job seekers, others push products and services which may not measure up to your expectations or needs. Further, what is best for someone else may not be good enough for you. As a consequence, it is important for you to know, with some degree of specificity, exactly what capabilities and features each site offers.

As with any other human endeavor, there is a wide range in the quality, usefulness and value of the services and support offered by employment Web-sites. For example,

- Some sites have been developed by experts in career counseling and job search, while others have been slapped together by individuals who have no experience or credentials in these areas. The former can provide you with information and advice that will help you build a successful and rewarding career; the latter can send you down blind alleys and even set you off in directions that can be harmful to your growth and progress in the world of work.

- Many of the sites in operation today are well capitalized and operated by established organizations, while others are very small and/or in financial jeopardy. If the former charges you a fee, you can count on receiving the product or service you purchased; the latter, however, may take your money and collapse before you ever receive anything of value.

- Some sites are especially innovative and creative while others offer the most rudimentary kind of on-line capability. The former can treat you to an experience that is entertaining, educational and engaging, while the latter is probably a waste of your time.

To help you navigate to those sites which will serve you best and avoid those which will not, you need to know:

Step 1: How to identify those sites that warrant your serious consideration and

Step 2: How to evaluate the capabilities offered by each site.

Acquiring this knowledge will enable you to select those sites which best support your job search and career objectives, both as they exist in the present and as they evolve in the future. In other words, it is a tool you can use time-and-again, throughout your worklife.

STEP 1: Identifying the Sites You Want to Evaluate

With more than 11,000 Web-sites offering employment services and information, it would easy to get frustrated or overwhelmed as you try to pinpoint those sites which are most likely to meet your needs. Even worse, sorting through the vast array of possibilities could cause you to overlook the one site that would be the best for you. As a consequence, it's important to try to narrow the universe of sites under consideration to a manageable number of prospects for in-depth evaluation. There are two methods you can use to make this initial selection:

- Sleuthing

- Guided tours

➤ **Sleuthing:** Sleuthing involves your doing your own research on the Internet to determine which sites are the best potential matches with the baseline site specifications you established in the previous chapter. It is a time-consuming activity, particularly if you're just learning how to navigate around the Internet and the World Wide Web, but it ensures that only your tastes and judgments are used to pick the contenders.

To begin your research project on the Internet, you must first select a search engine. Like a telescope, a search engine is your lens for peering into the vast expanse of cyberspace. As noted earlier, you can find a good on-line directory of search engines at *http://home.netscape.com/home/internet-search.html.* You simply need to pick the one application that seems most likely to do the job for you. Alternatively, if you don't feel comfortable making such a choice, I recommend that you use Yahoo! at *www.yahoo.com.* It will certainly get you started and give you plenty of investigatory horsepower.

To begin your search, you must designate which criteria you want your search engine to use. In this case, the most appropriate criteria are the category or categories of resources you specified in your baseline. For example, if you decided that the best site for you was one that provided access to jobs, use the term "job" or "jobs" as the key word for your search. Given the general nature of that term, however, it is likely to uncover a wide range of sites that deal with jobs in one way or another. Indeed, when I used this criterion in a search, I uncovered 69 categories and 4,382 specific sites which involved jobs of some kind. The categories ranged from Government: Employment: Local Government Jobs to Entertainment: Employment: Jobs, and the sites from aus.jobs, listing open positions in Australia, to Real Jobs for openings in real estate.

At this point, you have a choice; you can either move directly to the second step of the evaluation process and start your assessment of each site (4,382 is certainly a lot less than the entire population of 11,000+ sites) or you can let the computer narrow the field further to make your research effort more manageable (because 4,382 is still a very large number). If you decide to ask the computer to do a bit more of the legwork for you, you must add an additional level of detail to your search parameters. For example, you can tell the computer to look for all sites which deal with sales jobs. When I used that criteria in such a search, Yahoo! identified only one category and 99 site matches. The site matches ranged from the International Sales, Marketing and Management Job Site, for individuals with a background in international business, to the Retail Job Net, which is a data base of open positions in retail.

Once again, you have the option of taking the next step and investigating each of those 99 sites yourself or you can narrow your search parameters even further. For example, you might tell Yahoo! to look for all sites that deal with sales jobs and the title "manager" or sales jobs and the location "California." In either case, your goal is to narrow the range of alternatives so that you have the time and energy to give each a thorough and complete evaluation. Ultimately, you should try to identify a group of no more than 20 sites that you will evaluate in detail using the questionnaire in Step 2.

➤ **Guided Tours:** The other approach to narrowing the universe of prospective sites for your evaluation is to use a guided tour. Taking a guided tour enables you to rely on others for finding what's available on-line. These references will typically identify anywhere from dozens to hundreds of on-line employment sites and describe their capabilities. Most will also evaluate the resources that the sites offer and make a judgment as to their usefulness and reliability. Some of the guides are available on-line where they are called gateway sites, some appear in print as reference manuals and guide books and some are available in both forms. Some are free, and others are not. In either case, the upside to a guided tour is that it will save you time and can help you use the Internet and the World Wide Web effectively, even if you're unfamiliar with them. The downside is that you're dependent upon the capabilities and judgments of those who operate the gateway and write the guides, and their standards may be different than your own or the caliber of their work may be less than what you want.

There are a number of on-line references or gateways, including:

Guide Name	Internet Address	Developed By
Catapult	*http://www.jobweb.org/catapult/catapult.htm*	National Association of Colleges and Employers
JobHunt	*http://www.job-hunt.org*	Dane Spearing
The Net Guide	*http://www.washingtonpost.com/parachute*	Richard Nelson Bolles of *What Color is Your Parachute* fame
The Riley Guide	*http://www.dbm.com/jobguide*	Margaret F. Dikel (formerly Riley)

Similar guides or references are also available in print. I write one called the "Web-Site Review" which appears the *National Business Employment Weekly* (NBEW), published by Dow Jones. You can find all of my previous reviews in a feature called *Weddle's Web Guide* at the NBEW Web-site, *http://www.nbew.com/weddle.html*. In addition, I publish a special updated review of selected sites in a periodic newsletter which you can obtain by sending me an e-mail message at *pdweddle@worldnet.att.net*. Other print references include *CareerXroads*, written by Gerry Crispin and Mark Mehler, and updated regularly at their web site *http://www.careerxroads. com*; *The Guide to Internet Searching* by Margaret F. Riley; *Hook Up, Get Hired! The Internet Job Search Revolution* by Joyce Lain Kennedy; *Be Your Own Headhunter Online* by Pam Dixon and Sylvia Tiersten; and the chapter "Job-Hunting on The Internet" in the 1997 *What Color is Your Parachute* by Richard Nelson Bolles.

The best way to select a guide is to see how closely it mirrors the specifications in your baseline. The better the match, the more useful the guide will be in helping you to find the best alternative sites for you to evaluate. For an on-line guide, you can often determine what kind of data it provides by scanning its site. Usually, there is a table of contents or a top level summary of the categories that were used to organize the guide and a description of the information that is provided within each category. Alternatively, the guide may provide a site map which is, essentially, a top level outline of its content.

For a print guide, of course, the table of contents is a quick and easy way to assess the publication's scope and level of detail. In addition, the guide's author will often provide a summary of its features and content in an up-front Introduction. I also suggest that you check what others are saying about the guide. One easy way to get that information is to visit an on-line bookstore and read the reviews and comments about the book that are posted there.

Finally, as a corollary to your guided tour, you might also want to check with your professional association or alumni organization. These communities of interest have detailed knowledge of your occupational preparation or your professional credentials and, increasingly, a familiarity with those on-line employment resources which can be most helpful to you. The range of alternatives they have to suggest is likely to be much smaller than with the on-line and print guides, but they are far better informed about which employers like to recruit among the graduates of your alma mater or which employment sites specialize in your profession or area of expertise (and their Internet addresses). It's yet another way of using a "guide" to save you time and legwork.

STEP 2: Conducting Your Site Evaluations

The questionnaire below will help you to conduct a consistent and comprehensive evaluation of the Web-sites that you identified in Step 1. It will provide the detailed information you need both to determine the capabilities and features of each individual site accurately and to make reasonable comparisons of their benefits and value.

General

1. Which company, organization or individual sponsored the development of the site?

2. How long has the site been in operation?

3. Has the site received any awards or been selected for special recognition of any kind?

4. Have any professional associations, rating groups or other unbiased third parties endorsed the site or its services?

5. What is the look and feel of the site? Is it a visually appealing place to visit?

6. How clear are the site's instructions? Is it easy to use?

7. How efficient is the site to navigate? Is it easy to move between the various activities on the site?

8. Does the site offer any interactive experiences? Is it a fun and interesting?

Resume Circulation

1. How many resumes are posted in the site's database at this moment?

2. Are there any restrictions (i.e., membership in a group, alumni of a certain school, registration with the site) on who can post a resume?

3. Is there a fee charged to the individual to post a resume in the site's database?

4. Can you input your entire Internet resume in the site's database or are you limited to completing a short profile?

5. If you can input your entire Internet resume, how long will it be stored in the site's database?

6. Does the site permit employers to view the database directly or does it notify you first when a job opening matches your background?

7. If the site permits direct viewing of the database, does the site charge a fee for employers to see the resumes? Does it allow them to see the resume, but charge a fee to access the person's contact information?

8. In either case, how many employers paid this fee in the last 90 days?

9. Does the site provide testimonials from those who have stored their resume in the database?

10. Which employers have used the site to view and acquire candidate resumes from the database?

Assess Job Openings

1. What is the total number of job openings available in the site's database at this moment?

2. How many positions of the kind you are seeking (i.e., occupational field, industry and salary level) are in the site's database at this moment?

3. How often does the site update its job postings?

4. How long do the job openings stay posted in the database?

5. Where does the site obtain its job postings? Are any postings pulled from other Internet sites or from non-affiliated print publications?

6. Can the job database be searched by location? position title? salary level? industry?

7. Is there any fee charged to the individual to view the job openings?

8. How many employers posted a job opening in the site's database in the last year?

9. Does the site have any testimonials from employers who have used the site to fill job openings?

10. What are the names of some of the employers which have used the site to post job openings?

Information and Resources for Job Search and Career Management

1. Who develops the information and advice provided on the site?

2. What are the qualifications of these individuals/organizations in job search and career management?

3. How often is the information and other content updated?

4. Does the site include any or all of the following:
    _____ assessment instruments
    _____ career counseling
    _____ career and/or occupational information
    _____ directory of recruiters or employment agencies
    _____ employer profiles
    _____ hot links to employer sites
    _____ hot links to other sites with job search/career management resources
    _____ practice interviews/virtual interviews
    _____ job market information
    _____ job search counseling
    _____ job search tips
    _____ on-line job fairs
    _____ resume writing assistance
    _____ salary information and/or a salary calculator
    _____ schedule of job fairs and other employment events
    _____ other resources or services

5. Is there a fee to use any or all of the above resources?

Pay the Sites a Visit On-Line

If you used a guide in Step 1, you may be able to answer some of the above questions by referring to it. However, things change quickly in cyberspace, and any print guide is out of the date the moment it is published. Hence, the only way to answer most of these questions definitively is with a site visit, and even then, you may not be able to find all of the answers to all of the questions. Nevertheless, the more information you can obtain, the better able you will be to select the site or sites which will best serve your needs.

Perhaps more important, visiting each site is the only way for you to get a sense of its look and feel and to confirm exactly what resources it offers. In addition, you can test those resources, while you're there, to confirm that they will actually provide the caliber of support you're seeking with your job search. For example, is the interviewing assistance, provided by the site, the reprint of a journal article about the principles of a good interview or is it an interactive exercise that actually enables you to take a practice interview on-line? Unfortunately, there are no common definitions for "interviewing assistance" or the other services provided by the different employment sites, so the only way to know for sure is to check out each site's capabilities yourself.

The sites will give you three ways to learn about their features and capabilities when you visit them on-line:

1. The explanatory information provided throughout the site;

2. A set of up-to-date Frequently Asked Questions (FAQ's) and their answers; and

3. An e-mail interface which allows you to pose questions to the site's developer.

Finally, it is important to note that the above questionnaire is not fail safe. It will, however, give you the information you need to make a careful assessment of the different employment Web-sites in the marketplace. Virtually anyone with a personal computer can set themselves up in the on-line employment business, so such care is both appropriate and prudent. The effort is also worthwhile because a good employment Web-site can plug you into a whole new spectrum of employment opportunities and, through the efficiency and effectiveness of its technology, ensure that you are considered for each and every one of them.

16

Weddle's Picks: Twenty Top Notch Employment Web-Sites

The following employment Web-sites offer world class support to job seekers and others on-line, as of the date of this book's publication. Most of these sites offer significant capabilities in all three of the major areas of site operation: resume circulation, access to job postings and information and resources about job search and career management. As mentioned earlier, however, the Internet and World Wide Web change quickly and so can the capabilities and features of these and other sites. Hence, use your evaluation questionnaire to update the information below if the reality of your experience with a site differs from what I've described.

Further, there are many other very fine sites than those which I have mentioned here. Some are highly specialized and serve only a carefully defined segment of the workforce. Others have chosen to concentrate on one particular aspect of job search or career management or on services that are applicable to a limited number of people. Whatever the case, many of these sites are also worthy of your consideration.

The Key to Using Weddle's Picks

Like many popular travel guides, I've used a special format to describe the services and features of each employment Web-site in order to give you a lot of information in a short, succinct entry. As illustrated below, the site's name, the date it was first active on-line, and its Internet address or URL are presented first. Then, the site's key characteristics are briefly summarized. Finally, a series of symbols (letters and numbers) are used to detail the site's capabilities on four lines:

Line 1: Resume Circulation
Line 2: Access to Job Openings
Line 3: The Kinds of Job Openings in the Site's Database
Line 4: Information and Resources

For example:

America's Employers   1995   http://www.americasemployers.com
Developed by the Career Relocation Corporation of America, America's Employers describes itself as a site which "guides the job seeker through every aspect of the job campaign in a straightforward and easy-to-use format."
  1:   RP, 90 + 90 optional renewal
  2:   JF, JD, ++++, 7
  3:   FA, HT, MG
  4:   CH, CC, CI, DR, EP, HE, HL, JC, JI, RW

The following key is a guide to using these symbols.

Weddle's Guide to Top Notch Employment Web-Sites

Line 1: Resume Circulation

RE	...	site accepts resumes for posting in a database on the site
RF	...	site charges a fee to post your resume or profile
RG	...	you must register with the site to post your resume
RN	...	site does not accept resumes for posting on the site
RP	...	site does not accept resumes but does allow you to post a profile of your credentials
RR	...	there is a restriction on who can post a resume on the site
90	...	the period of time you can post your resume in days
IN	...	your resume can be posted for an indefinite period

Line 2: Access to Job Openings

JB	...	jobs are posted on a scrolling bulletin board
JD	...	jobs are posted in a searchable database

JF	...	the site posts full time job openings in its database
JN	...	the site does not post job openings on the site
JP	...	the site posts contract, contingent, project & non-full time job openings
+	...	the site's database currently holds 0-1,000 jobs
++	...	the site's database currently holds 1,001-10,000 jobs
+++	...	the site's database currently holds 10,001-30,000 jobs
++++	...	the site's database currently holds 30,001-50,000 jobs
+++++	...	the site's database currently holds 50,000+ jobs
14	...	how frequently job openings are updated in days

Line 3: The Kinds of Job Openings in the Site's Database

AD	...	administrative	HT	...	high tech
CM	...	communication	IS	...	info systems
CR	...	computer-related	IT	...	info technology
DP	...	data processing	MG	...	management
EN	...	engineering	PG	...	programmers
FA	...	finance/accounting	SM	...	sales/marketing
UNK	...	site does not collect/report this information			

Line 4: Information & Resources

AN	...	site automatically notifies you when your resume matches a job opening
AS	...	site offers assessment instruments
CC	...	site offers career counseling
CH	...	site offers chats and bulletin boards about job search/career management
CI	...	site offers career/occupational information
DR	...	site offers a directory of recruiters or employment agencies
EP	...	site offers employer profiles/contact or other information
HE	...	site offers hot links to employers' Web-sites
HL	...	site offers hot links to other employment Web-sites
IF	...	site charges a fee for access to some or all of its information and resources
JC	...	site offers job search counseling
JI	...	site offers job market/search information
PI	...	site offers practice/virtual interviews
RW	...	site offers resume writing assistance/information
SC	...	site offers schedule of/connection to job fairs or other employment events
SI	...	site offers salary information/calculator

> **The following profiles were compiled from data provided by the site operators and/or their designated representatives and from my own visits to each Web-site. Every effort was made to ensure the accuracy of the information presented in the profiles, as of the date of its publication.**

America's Employers   1995   http://www.americasemployers.com
Developed by the Career Relocation Corporation of America, America's Employers describes itself as a site which "guides the job seeker through every aspect of the job campaign in a straightforward and easy-to-use format."

    1:   RP, 90 + 90 optional renewal
    2:   JF, JD, ++++, 7
    3:   FA, HT, MG
    4:   CH, CC, CI, DR, EP, HE, HL, JC, JI, RW

America's Job Bank   1995   http://www.ajb.dni.us
Developed by the U.S. Department of Labor and the states' public employment service agencies, America's Job Bank describes itself as "a nationwide database of electronic resumes that can be searched electronically by employers to find qualified candidates for their job openings."

    1:   RN/Expected in 1998 @ America's Talent Bank at http://www.atb.org
    2:   JF, JD, +++++, 1
    3:   AD, CR, EN, IT
    4:   CI, EP, HE, HL, JI, RW, SI

Best Jobs U.S.A.   1996   http://www.bestjobsusa.com
Developed by Recourse Communications, Inc., Best Jobs U.S.A. describes itself as "a premier employment web site providing vast resources, tools, and information for career advancement and mastery of today's workplace issues."

    1:   RE, 365
    2:   JF, JD, +++, 1
    3:   CR, EN, IT, SM
    4:   CI, EP, HE, HL, JI, SC, SI

CareerBuilder.com   **1996**   **http://careerbuilder.com**
Developed by CareerBuilder, Inc., CareerBuilder.com describes itself as "unique from a technology standpoint but also content."

    1:   RN
    2:   JF, JD, ++, 1
    3:   AD, HT, SM
    4:   AN, AS, CC, CH, CI, EP, HE, HL, JC, JI, RW, SI

CareerCity   **1995**   **http://www.careercity.com**
Developed by Adams Media Corporation, CareerCity describes itself as "a complete career center, with over 200 career-guiding articles and advice from best-selling authors, and self-assessment quizzes."

    1:   RE, 120
    2:   JF, JD, +++++, 1
    3:   CR, EN, MG
    4:   AS, CI, EP, HL, JI, PI, RW, SC, SI

CareerMagazine   **1994**   **http://careermag.com**
Developed by NCS, Inc., CareerMagazine describes itself as "a complete career resource center in a magazine format."

    1:   RE, 180
    2:   JF, JB, +++, 1
    3:   EN, PG, SM
    4:   CH, CI, DR, EP, HE, HL, JI, RW, SC, SI

CareerMosaic   **1994**   **http://www.careermosaic.com**
Developed by Bernard Hodes Advertising, Career Mosaic describes itself as "the first site on the World Wide Web devoted to employment and foremost in integrating new features that make job search easier and more cost-effective."

1:   RE, 120
2:   JF, JD, +++++, 1
3:   EN, IT, SM
4:   CI, EP, HE, HL, JI, RW, SC, SI

CareerPath   **1995**   **http://careerpath.com**

Developed by a consortium of major newspapers around the country, CareerPath describes itself as "the preeminent career management site on the Internet, combining the breadth and depth of over 200,000 current classified job listings from over 50 newspapers across the United States."

1:   RP, 180
2:   JF, JP, JD, +++++, 1
3:   CR, EN, MG
4:   CI, EP, RW, SI

Careers.wsj.com   **1997**   **http://www.careers.wsj.com**

Developed by Dow Jones & Company, Inc., Careers.wsj.com describes itself as a free site featuring "favorite columns and in-depth analysis of employment issues from *The Wall Street Journal*, practical advice articles and salary data from the *National Business Employment Weekly*."

1:   RN
2:   JF, JD, +++, 7
3:   MG, SM, HT
4:   CC, CH, CI, DR, EP, HE, HL, JC, JI, RW, SI

CareerWeb   **1995**   **http://www.cweb.com**

Developed by Landmark Communications, Inc, CareerWeb describes itself as a site which "publishes recruitment advertising on the Internet for technical, professional and managerial jobs."

1:   RE, 90
2:   JF, JD, +++, 1

3:   EN, IS, SM
4:   AN, AS, CC, CI, EP, HE, HL, JI, SC, SI

Contract Employment Connection 1993   **http://www.ntes.com**
Developed by National Technical Employment Services (NTES), the
Contract Employment Connection describes itself as another feature of
NTES, which was "founded in 1983 to assist the Contract Professional in
maintaining employment in the temporary job market through services and
publications."

1:   RE, RR, IN
2:   JP, JD, +, 1
3:   EN, IT, MG
4:   CI, DR, HL, SI

E.Span   **1994**   **http://www.espan.com**
Developed by E.span, this site states that it "helps viewers zero in on
information, job seekers zero in on positions and employers/recruiters zero
in on prime candidates."

1:   RE, 270
2:   JF, JD, +++, 1
3:   EN, IS, MG
4:   AN, CI, HE, HL, JI, RW, SC, SI

JobTrak   **1994**   **http://www.jobtrak.com**
Developed by JOBTRAK Corporation, JOBTRAK describes itself as "the
only site to have formed unique partnerships with over 700 college and
university career centers, MBA programs and alumni associations."

1:   RP, RR, 90
2:   JF, JP, JD, ++++, 1
3:   CR, MG, SM
4:   AS, CC, CH, CI, EP, HE, HL, JC, JI, RW, SC, SI

The Monster Board   **1995**   **http://www.monster.com**

Developed by TMP Worldwide, The Monster Board describes itself as "the premier career site on the Internet, connecting top employers with job seekers online."

1:   RE, 365
2:   JF, JD, +++, 1
3:   EN, IS, FA, SM
4:   AN, CC, CI, EP, HE, HL, JC, JI, RW, SC, SI

NationJob Network   **1995**   **http://www.nationjob.com**

Developed by NationJob, Inc., NationJob Network states that it "lists thousands of detailed, current jobs and employer profiles. Our work with communities and newspapers as well as individual employers results in many job listings that aren't available anywhere else."

1:   RP, RG, IN
2:   JF, JD, ++, 1
3:   UNK
4:   AN, EP, HE

Online Career Center   **1993**   **http://www.occ.com**

Originally developed through corporate sponsorship and now owned by TMP Worldwide, the Online Career Center describes itself as "the first and most frequently accessed career site."

1:   RE, 90
2:   JF, JD, +++++, 1
3:   HT, IS, IT, MG, SM
4:   CH, CI, EP, HL, JI, RW, SC, SI

TAPS.com   **1995**   **http://www.taps.com**

Developed by Internet Appointments, Ltd., TAPS.com describes itself as "Europe's largest job site carrying up to 60% of United Kingdom and European IT and other positions at any one time by volume."

1:   RP, RG, IN
2:   JF, JP, JD, ++, 1
3:   IT
4:   AN, CC, CI, DR, EP, HL, JI

Town Online Working   1996   http://www.townonline.com/working
Developed by the Community Newspaper Company, Town Online Working
states that it "features state-of-the-art intelligent agent functionalities to
match job seekers to job openings, and employers to candidates."

1:   RE, RP, 365
2:   JF, JD, +, 7
3:   AD, IS, PG, SM
4:   AN, CC, CH, CI, EP, HL, JC, JI, SC, SI

Westech Virtual Job Fair   1994   http://www.vjf.com
Developed by Westech ExpoCorp, Westech Virtual Job Fair describes itself
as "a complete career resource with jobs, career advice, job fair info, and
links to other resources."

1:   RE, RR, 60
2:   JF, JD, +++, 1
3:   EN, IS, SM
4:   CI, EP, HE, HL, JI, RW, SC, SI

World.Hire ONLINE   1996   http://www.world.hire.com
Developed by World.hire, World.hire ONLINE describes itself as "a one-
stop web site for job seekers and people looking for career advice."

1:   RP, 180
2:   JF, JD, +, 30
3:   EN, IT, MG
4:   AN, CI, DR, HL, JI, RW, SC, SI

Career Resources

C ontact Impact Publications to receive a free annotated listing of career resources or visit their World Wide Web (Internet) site for a complete listing of career resources: *http://www.impactpublications.com.*
The following career resources are available directly from Impact Publications. Complete this form or list the titles, include postage (see formula at the end), enclose payment, and send your order to:

IMPACT PUBLICATIONS
9104-N Manassas Drive
Manassas Park, VA 20111-5211
Tel. 703/361-7300 or Fax 703/335-9486
E-mail: *impactp@impactpublications.com*

Orders from individuals must be prepaid by check, moneyorder, Visa, MasterCard, or American Express. We accept telephone, fax, and e-mail orders.

Qty.	TITLES	Price	TOTAL
Internet Resumes, Job Finding, and Recruitment			
___	CareerXroads 1998	$22.95	___
___	Employer's Guide to Recruiting on the Internet	$24.95	___
___	Guide to Internet Job Finding	$14.95	___
___	How to Get Your Dream Job Using the Web	$29.99	___
___	Internet Resumes	$14.95	___
___	Resumes in Cyberspace	$17.95	___
Resumes			
___	100 Winning Resumes For $100,000+ Jobs	$24.95	___
___	101 Best Resumes	$10.95	___
___	175 High-Impact Resumes	$10.95	___
___	1500+ KeyWords for $100,000+ Jobs	$14.95	___
___	Adams Resume Almanac	$10.95	___
___	America's Top Resumes For America's Top Jobs	$19.95	___

____ Asher's Bible of Executive Resumes $29.95 ____
____ Best Resumes For $75,000+ Executive Jobs $14.95 ____
____ Building a Great Resume $15.00 ____
____ Complete Idiot's Guide to Crafting the Perfect Resume $16.95 ____
____ Designing the Perfect Resume $12.95 ____
____ Dynamite Resumes $14.95 ____
____ Encyclopedia of Job-Winning Resumes $16.95 ____
____ Gallery of Best Resumes $16.95 ____
____ Gallery of Best Resumes For Two-Year Degree Graduates $14.95 ____
____ High Impact Resumes and Letters $19.95 ____
____ How to Prepare Your Curriculum Vitae $14.95 ____
____ Just Resumes $11.95 ____
____ New Perfect Resume $10.95 ____
____ Portfolio Power $14.95 ____
____ Real-Life Resumes That Work! $12.95 ____
____ Resume Catalog $15.95 ____
____ Resume Pro $24.95 ____
____ Resume Shortcuts $14.95 ____
____ Resume Winners From the Pros $17.95 ____
____ Resumes & Job Search Letters For Transitioning Military Personnel $17.95 ____
____ Resumes For Dummies $12.99 ____
____ Resumes For the Healthcare Professional $12.95 ____
____ Resumes For People Who Hate to Write Resumes $12.95 ____
____ Resumes For Re-Entry: A Woman's Handbook $10.95 ____
____ Resumes That Knock 'Em Dead $10.95 ____
____ Sure-Hire Resumes $14.95 ____

Resume Books With Computer Disk

____ Adams Resume Almanac With Disk $19.95 ____
____ New 90-Minute Resume $15.95 ____
____ Ready-to-Go Resumes $16.95 ____

Resume CD-ROMs

____ Adams JobBank Fast Resume Suite $49.95 ____
____ ResumeMaker $49.95 ____
____ Win-Way Resume 4.0 $69.95 ____

Cover Letters

____ 175 High-Impact Cover Letters $10.95 ____
____ 200 Letters For Job Hunters $19.95 ____
____ 201 Dynamite Job Search Letters $19.95 ____
____ 201 Killer Cover Letters $16.95 ____
____ 201 Winning Cover Letters For $100,000+ Jobs $24.95 ____
____ Adams Cover Letter Almanac and Disk $19.95 ____
____ Cover Letters For Dummies $12.99 ____
____ Cover Letters That Knock 'Em Dead $10.95 ____
____ Dynamite Cover Letters $14.95 ____
____ Perfect Cover Letter $10.95 ____

Interviews, Networking, and Salary Negotiations

___ 101 Dynamite Answers to Interview Questions	$12.95	___
___ 101 Dynamite Questions to Ask At Your Job Interview	$14.95	___
___ 111 Dynamite Ways to Ace Your Job Interview	$13.95	___
___ 201 Answers to the Toughest Job Interview Questions	$10.95	___
___ Adams Job Interview Almanacs	$10.95	___
___ Dynamite Networking For Dynamite Jobs	$15.95	___
___ Dynamite Salary Negotiation	$15.95	___
___ Great Connections	$19.95	___
___ How to Work a Room	$9.95	___
___ Interview For Success	$15.95	___
___ Job Interviews For Dummies	$12.99	___
___ Power Schmoozing	$12.95	___
___ The Secrets of Savvy Networking	$11.99	___
___ What Do I Say Next?	$20.00	___

SUBTOTAL -- ___

Virginia residents add 4½% sales tax ___

POSTAGE/HANDLING ($5.00 for first
title plus 8% of SUBTOTAL over $30) $5.00

8% of SUBTOTAL over $30 --- ___

TOTAL ENCLOSED --- ___

NAME _____

ADDRESS _____

_____

_____

❑ I enclose check/moneyorder for $ _____ made payable to IMPACT
PUBLICATIONS.

❑ Please charge $ _____ to my credit card:

❑ Visa   ❑ MasterCard   ❑ American Express   ❑ Discover

Card # _____

Expiration date: _____/_____

Signature _____

The On-Line Superstore & Warehouse

Hundreds of Terrific Career Resources Conveniently Available On the World Wide Web 24-Hours a Day, 365 Days a Year!

Ever wanted to know what are the newest and best books, directories, newsletters, wall charts, training programs, videos, CD-ROMs, computer software, and kits available to help you land a job, negotiate a higher salary, or start your own business? What about finding a job in Asia or relocating to San Francisco? Are you curious about how to find a job 24-hours a day by using the Internet or what to do after you leave the military? Trying to keep up-to-date on the latest career resources but not able to find the latest catalogs, brochures, or newsletters on today's "best of the best" resources?

Welcome to the first virtual career resource center/bookstore on the Internet. Now you're only a "click" away with Impact Publication's electronic solution to the resource challenge. Impact Publications, one of the nation's leading publishers and distributors of career resources, has launched its comprehensive "Career Superstore and Warehouse" on the Internet. The bookstore is jam-packed with the latest resources focusing on several key career areas:

- Alternative jobs and careers
- Self-assessment
- Career planning and job search
- Employers
- Relocation and cities
- Resumes
- Cover letters
- Dress, image, and etiquette
- Education
- Telephone
- Military
- Salaries
- Interviewing
- Nonprofits

- Empowerment
- Self-esteem
- Goal setting
- Executive recruiters
- Entrepreneurship
- Government
- Networking
- Electronic job search
- International jobs
- Travel
- Law
- Training and presentations
- Minorities
- Physically challenged

"This is more than just a bookstore offering lots of product," say Drs. Ron and Caryl Krannich, two of the nation's leading career experts and authors and developers of this on-line bookstore. *"We're an important resource center for libraries, corporations, government, educators, trainers, and career counselors who are constantly defining and redefining this dynamic field. Of the thousands of career resources we review each year, we only select the 'best of the best.'"*

Visit this rich site and you'll quickly discover just about everything you ever wanted to know about finding jobs, changing careers, and starting your own business—including many useful resources that are difficult to find in local bookstores and libraries. The site also includes what's new and hot, tips for success, monthly specials, and a "Military Career Transition Center." Impact's Web address is:

http://www.impactpublications.com